VOM Books

The publishing division of

Serving persecuted Christians since 1967

vom.org

What people are saying about...

I Am N

"There is no doubt that radical Islam is one of the greatest challenges facing the church today. These inspiring accounts of the persecuted church will move you to tears and then drive you to your knees. We all have a scriptural responsibility to stand up for and stand with our brothers and sisters who are going through the fire. Don't let the horrors described here intimidate you, because fear is a terrorist's greatest weapon. Instead, be stirred up to pray that the Holy Spirit may give you boldness to speak out, to take action, to get involved. Similarly, don't let these indescribable crimes fill you with hate for Muslims. Many Muslims would join us in condemning these atrocities. We are called to follow our Savior in loving our enemies, serving their needs, and having compassion on their blindness. The sacrificial faith of the suffering saints described in this book show us all how we are to respond at this time of crisis, courageously daring to love Muslims with the love of Christ."

JULYAN LIDSTONE
Operation Mobilization (OM)

"VOM's *I Am N* is a challenging mosaic of stories that remind us of normal Christianity, faith that is lived out in persecution. There are a lot of reminders within the pages of this book. We are reminded that there are no such entities as a 'free church' or a 'persecuted church'; there is simply *one church*, always persecuted and free. The church in persecution teaches us how to pray, not that their persecution might end but that they might be obedient through their sufferings. This is a prayer that prays both halves of the prayer of Jesus. It is always appropriate to pray for 'let this cup pass' while never forgetting to pray to the Father that 'thy will be done.'"

Nik Ripken
International Mission Board of the Southern Baptist Convention
Author of *The Insanity of God* and *The Insanity of Obedience*

"Islamic terrorism is often the lead news story of the day, but Jesus promised to build his church and that the gates of hell would not prevail against it. So although terrorism grabs the headlines, Jesus's followers are flourishing right in the heart of the danger. *I Am N* was written to tell the stories of brave believers on the frontlines of today's raging spiritual battle. Their courage will inspire you to think differently, live differently, and your heart will be refreshed as you get to know them. I believe they have become the new face of Christianity and we can learn much from them. The word *retreat* is foreign to the gospel. Brothers and sisters who live in harm's way today are in no way waving white flags. Instead, they're yelling 'Charge' and taking the gospel to the ends of the earth even if it costs them their lives."

Tom Doyle, e3 Partners
Author of *Killing Christians: Living the Faith*
Where It's Not Safe to Believe

"Instability is our new normal. The gospel must ever be preached under pressure, and we must give up the idea that we can truly stand up for Jesus anywhere in the world without suffering for him. The only people in the world who can avoid the equal and opposite errors of Islamophobia and naive accommodation are the followers of Jesus who love Jesus enough to share in his sufferings and who love Muslims enough to suffer and die for them."

DICK BROGDEN

Assemblies of God World Missions

Author of *Live Dead Joy: 365 Days of Living and Dying with Jesus*

"The further we are removed from the suffering of others, the easier it is to do nothing. We must not allow ourselves that option. Through these stories, please allow yourself to draw near to our persecuted brothers and sisters. In my role as a leader of a missions agency reaching out to Muslim people, I've been pulled into the suffering. Personal friends have been beaten, imprisoned, tortured, or killed. My tears, sleepless nights, and prayers didn't seem enough. I am extremely grateful for a partnership we now have with The Voice of the Martyrs. In practical ways they are helping us deal with the persecution and showing us how to get back up and press on with the good news of God's love through Jesus. This book will help us all respond in compassion."

KEVIN

Missions executive with more than thirty years of service in restricted and least-reached nations

"It has been our honor and privilege to pray, weep, and serve alongside brothers and sisters who have suffered for Christ at the hands of their families, neighbors, and governments. As we recall their faces and tell their stories, we join the apostle Paul in saying, 'I thank my God every time I remember you … I always pray with joy because of your partnership in the gospel from the first day until now' (Philippians 1:3–5). God is at work in extraordinary ways in the midst of the worst possible terror, oppression, and violence. The Christians you will meet in this book reveal a hope and strength that is both supernatural and eternal. These family members have completely abandoned their personal agendas and are learning to trust God absolutely. We have much to learn from their example."

COLE RICHARDS
President, The Voice of the Martyrs

◄ REVISED AND UPDATED ►

i am n

*Inspiring Stories of Christians
Facing Islamic Extremists*

the voice of the martyrs

VOMBOOKS
The Voice of the Martyrs

I Am N
Published by VOM Books
A division of The Voice of the Martyrs
1815 SE Bison Rd.
Bartlesville, OK 74006

Original edition published in 2016 by David C Cook (DCC)

Second edition published in 2024 by VOM Books

Library of Congress Control Number: 2023946067
Paperback: 978-0-88264-255-0
eBook: 978-0-88264-256-7
Audiobook: 978-0-88264-257-4

New stories for the 2024 Revised and Updated Edition by
The Voice of the Martyrs with Mikal Keefer
Edited by Sheryl Martin Hash
Interior layout by Genesis Group

Details in some stories have been changed to protect
the identities of the persons involved.

Printed in the United States of America

202307p007a1

*Remember those who are in prison, as though
in prison with them, and those who are
mistreated, since you also are in the body.*

HEBREWS 13:3

CONTENTS

INTRODUCTION

"I Am N?" What Does That Mean?

When militants from the self-proclaimed Islamic State of Iraq and Syria (ISIS) moved into northern Iraq in 2014, they began identifying Christian-owned property. Families found the Arabic letter ن (*nun*, *noon*), or *n*, painted on their homes and churches. This single letter conveyed the powerful accusation that the occupants were "Nazarenes," people who followed Jesus of Nazareth rather than Islam. To be labeled "n" in a community invaded by Muslim extremists was to be thrust into a crisis of spiritual identity.

The militants gave all Christians until July 19 to convert to Islam, pay a high tax (called a *jizyah*), leave the city, or be killed. Thousands chose to flee, leaving everything they owned behind. Along the way, families encountered roadblock after roadblock of ISIS soldiers guarding their conquered territory. The soldiers robbed them, taking wedding rings and ripping passports in half before the horrified owners' eyes. In some cases, soldiers told people to strip, and then robbed them of even their clothing.

Many of the refugees fled to Kurdistan, a semi-autonomous region of Iraq that ISIS had not yet penetrated, and specifically to the city of Erbil. And when they arrived, they learned the city was crowded with refugees, as Erbil was already hosting more than two hundred thousand Syrian refugees who had fled the civil war in their country. Families were camped in any available space—parks, church yards, and half-constructed buildings.

More than seven hundred thousand people fled to Kurdistan after the ISIS takeover of Mosul, and others fled to surrounding countries. The refugees included Muslims, Christians, and others, but only Christians were issued the July 19 ultimatum.

One Christian man from Mosul, who was unaware of the ultimatum, heard bombs going off the night of July 19 and soon realized that only Christian homes were being destroyed. He quickly gathered his wife and daughter, and they ran from their home. They, too, were among the Christians who were robbed, stripped, and humiliated at ISIS checkpoints.

The refugees from Mosul lost more than just homes and possessions. Some civilians lost their lives during the ISIS invasion. Others lost hope for their future. One Christian woman had just completed four years of college and was scheduled to take her final exam on July 20. She missed her exam, and all records at the university were likely destroyed by ISIS.

But the crisis also created opportunities for Christians to demonstrate the love of Christ. One Christian businessman in Erbil cleared out an office building he owned so refugees from Mosul could live there.

And as always, God provided hope in this massive crisis.

One refugee told a VOM worker, "If Islam is like [ISIS], then I don't want to be a Muslim." That man and other former Muslims have turned to Christ through the witness of a team of evangelists in the area.

As for the Christians who fled Mosul, those who put their hope in Christ knew they were not defeated. One family said, "We have lost all our possessions, but we still have our faith in Jesus. No one can take that away from us."

And they said this in light of the reality that their situation would not be temporary; their life circumstances on this earth would be unlikely to improve—ever![1]

Their courageous, steadfast commitment to God in the face of persecution provides followers of Christ all over the world with a powerful picture of what being "n" is all about. They willingly sacrifice everything they have in this world in order to fulfill God's calling to obey and serve him. Like the heroes of the faith whose stories we read in the Bible and in the record of church history, they are living out Paul's words in Philippians 3:8: "Indeed, I count everything as loss because of the surpassing worth of knowing Christ Jesus my Lord. For his sake I have suffered the loss of all things and count them as rubbish, in order that I may gain Christ."

---

1.   In 2017, military forces defeated ISIS, pushing them out of Mosul. Some refugees were able to return; others have not.

Stories That Inspire Response

This book shares the stories of Christians who have suffered persecution not only in Mosul, Iraq, but also a number of other countries where they face Islamic extremists. They live in communities and nations where it is difficult and dangerous to follow Christ. Their sacrifice, courage, joy, perseverance, forgiveness, and faithfulness in the face of opposition—and even death—are a powerful testimony to our loving God, whose grace reaches out to save all sinners and empowers those who place their trust in Jesus as Savior and Lord to live as obedient biblical disciples.

We pray the exemplary witness of these persecuted believers will inspire you to join them in loving Muslims and working to see them come to Christ in your own community. We need their example of faithfulness in the face of persecution to encourage us in our walk with the Lord (Hebrews 12:1–2).

Knowing that these true accounts of actual incidents happened to real people is unsettling. Some are troubling; others are truly horrifying. For every one of these stories, there are hundreds more that will never be known.

As you read their stories, we encourage you to stand with them in frequent prayer. They will know they are not alone in their efforts to share the love of Jesus—even when the cost to them or their loved ones is beatings, torture, or death. But more importantly, it is affirmation that we are all part of the global body of Christ!

As you get to know our persecuted brothers and sisters in Christ, you will discover they are not "super Christians" who have somehow attained a higher level of godliness. They are people just like us. They feel deep anguish when their children are taken away, their husbands are killed, their sons are attacked, their wives are raped, and their daughters are forced into sexual slavery. They face uncertainty and fear when they are kicked out of their families, lose their jobs, and are cast out of their communities because they follow Jesus.

To thrive while enduring such suffering, they pray for courage, faith, and endurance. They tenaciously cling to and obey the Word of God, trusting in his loving, faithful character and the certainty of heaven. Having lost everything of value in this world, they learn to trust that God is in control, no matter what.

As our persecuted brothers and sisters in Christ walk this path, they see their circumstances through God's eternal perspective. That perspective leads them to view themselves among those who serve on the frontlines as God accomplishes his purposes in the midst of evil and chaos. Their eyes are open to see that ISIS and other Islamic extremists are not able to thwart God's eternal plan.

The world is not just one big chaotic mess. God is at work powerfully and strategically. The very suffering of our persecuted brothers and sisters is creating a deep hunger for the truth of Jesus Christ among many moderate Muslims who express deep hurt, regret, and even anger over the atrocities committed by Islamic extremists. They are looking for a hope that is unfamiliar to the Islam they are witnessing. Like the refugee you read about earlier, some even say, "We've read the Quran and know that Muhammad himself committed such atrocities. Now we want to learn about Christianity—about Jesus, about the Bible. Please tell us more."

Seizing the opportunity, these precious followers of Christ boldly proclaim, "I am n." Counting the cost, they stand firm, faithfully sharing the message of God's grace to a world that desperately needs him. How can we let them stand alone or suffer in silence? Will we let their stories deepen our commitment to Christ and his Great Commission? Will we join them in saying, "I am n"?

THE VOICE OF THE MARTYRS

Part I

SACRIFICE

And he said to all, "If anyone would come after me, let him deny himself and take up his cross daily and follow me."

LUKE 9:23

Sacrifice is never far from the hearts and minds of biblical disciples who are persecuted by Islamic extremists. For them, the consequences of obedience to Christ are clear. The sacrifices they make are certain and well defined. Before they choose Jesus as Lord and Savior, they count the cost of being his disciple. They know that once their faith becomes visible to others, persecution will come. They expect it, and they accept it. They understand Paul's words in Romans 12:1 in a way few of us can: "I appeal to you therefore, brothers, by the mercies of God, to present your bodies as a living sacrifice." And they decide—every day—to make that personal sacrifice.

They witness for Jesus in hostile communities rather than fleeing to safer countries—and are often arrested, jailed, beaten, tortured, or killed. They prepare their children for persecution, and even martyrdom, as the consequence of living out their faith in Jesus Christ.

They face daily beatings or even expulsion from their once-protective Muslim families through which all of life's opportunities flow: food, shelter, education, marriage, and work.

Their homes and possessions are confiscated or destroyed, driving them to live in refugee camps where they have nothing to call their own and no promise of food, shelter, or safety for tomorrow.

Yet our brothers and sisters who follow Christ in such countries proclaim, through word and action, "It's worth it. We are disciples of Jesus Christ. We will remain committed to God and his kingdom no matter what sacrifices are required. We are called to make disciples. Regardless of what happens, we have hope because Jesus promised to prepare a place for us where we will be with him forever."

1

THE DAY ISIS
ARRIVED IN MOSUL

Abu Fadi
Iraq

That day in June 2014 broke like almost any other day in Mosul, Iraq: hot, dusty, and teeming with people, traffic, and trade. People flocked to marketplaces in Iraq's second-largest city. Horns honked amid the pent-up traffic. As the day progressed, the din of street-side chatter rose appreciably. By noon, it sounded like a cacophony of blackbirds chattering among themselves.

That's when Abu Fadi, a sixty-five-year-old Mosul native living just miles from the city, received the phone call that changed everything. For some, the phone call marked the beginning of the end of life as they knew it—and in some cases, the end of their very lives.

"Abu," said a friend in Arabic, "ISIS is coming. We have heard from someone we trust. Today is the day."

The rumor mill had been churning for weeks that self-proclaimed ISIS terrorists, who had been ravaging cities elsewhere in Iraq, would take Mosul next. That's where Abu's mother, Sara, and sister, Dleen, lived. As Christians, they would be in grave danger. ISIS hated many people in the world, but especially Christians. The ultimatum to followers of Jesus? Convert to Islam, pay an outlandishly high tax, leave, or be killed.

"How can we hope to get my mother and sister out?" asked Abu. Both women were disabled and in wheelchairs.

"It will not be easy," his friend stated. "And if Mosul falls, can your city be far behind? We must pray very hard, Abu. We must—"

Baroom.

An ISIS military water tanker, rigged with explosives, blew up near the Mosul Hotel where government security officers were stationed. Abu's friend hung up the phone. Chaos descended on Mosul.

Armored vehicles rumbled down streets. Gunfire broke out. A woman who had planned to celebrate this day as her wedding day died in a blast.

ISIS fighters ripped down the cross on the Syriac Orthodox cathedral of Mar[1] Afram. They replaced the cross with loudspeakers proclaiming that Islam, not Jesus, was the way.

Pandemonium reigned. People dragged possessions to cars. Traffic jams closed roads. Screams of panic echoed. Amid it all,

1.   Mar means "saint" or "martyr" in Aramaic.

Abu received sporadic phone reports from his friend in Mosul, who at one point said, "The Iraqi army is now fleeing the city."

During the following weeks, Abu secured permission from an ISIS judge to permit his mother and sister to stay in Mosul. A few weeks after taking Mosul, ISIS swept into Abu's city, just as he had feared. More Christians hastily packed and fled, but Abu and his wife, Rukia, could not leave Sara and Dleen.

For sixteen days, ISIS occupied the area where Abu lived—sixteen days that to Abu seemed like sixteen years.

"Please come get me, Abu," pleaded his mother during yet another phone call from Mosul. "It is not safe here. You must—"

A man's hardened voice cut in on the line. "Let me state it more clearly," the ISIS soldier declared. "If you do not come get these two infidel dogs, they will either be converted to Islam with guns at their heads or thrown onto the street."

Abu had no chance to get his mother that day because he'd be going against the surge of frantic people escaping the city. Both women were allowed to stay with a Muslim neighbor for the night, but the ISIS soldier confiscated their house, pulled a can of spray paint from a bag, and tagged the front of the house with ن—an Arabic *n* for "Nazarene"—*Christians live here. Property of the Islamic State.*

Unable to go to his mother and sister, Abu arranged for a Muslim friend to drive the women to him. Once they arrived, Abu and the women could flee from there. Like almost forty thousand others who fled the purge in Mosul and the surrounding area, they crammed the few possessions they could fit into the car and headed east for relative safety in the city of Erbil, sixty miles away.

Soon Abu and his family arrived at the first checkpoint. Cars weighed down to their struts with people and their possessions inched forward in dozens of lines. Exhaust polluted the air. ISIS guards stood with firearms and swords. Abu had prayed about this moment—for courage to stand for his beliefs.

"Who are you?" a guard asked.

"We are Christians leaving Mosul, because we are not permitted to stay in this Muslim land," Abu replied.

The guard, now joined by others, refused to let the family pass. Instead, they placed a call to superiors. Thirty minutes later, two shiny SUVs arrived. Young men brandishing new, expensive firearms stepped out and began questioning the family.

Abu answered honestly: "Yes, we are Christians."

"Leaving is no longer an option for you and the rest of your infidel family," said the leader. "Convert to Islam or be killed. It is that simple. It is an easy choice, no?"

Abu begged the men to let his family proceed. He referred to passages in the Quran that allow Christians to live if they pay the *jizya* (Islamic tax). For ninety agonizing minutes the discussion continued, as if a bomb were ticking and destined to go off any second. As they talked, an ISIS fighter wielding a sword circled Abu, ready to strike if he tried to run.

"Enough," declared the leader. He grabbed Abu by the arm and led him away as his wife, mother, and sister wept, pleaded, and prayed. "Prepare to die," he said, pushing Abu to his knees. "Last chance. Will you convert to Islam?"

Abu looked back to the three women, then heavenward. He prayed for strength, wisdom, and courage. Even though he felt weak and expected the sword to plunge into him at any moment, he sensed God's peace strengthening him. "No, I will not be a Muslim," he stated. "I do *not* denounce Jesus."

The man raised his sword. Abu bowed his head, closed his eyes, and prayed. When he heard another vehicle arrive, he exhaled. Another black SUV. Out came another ISIS official, who inquired about the situation and then walked over to Abu.

"I have a message for you to deliver to your church leaders as you leave our land," he said. "We are victorious. And we will follow you Christians all over the world. We will reach the Vatican and convert the pope to Islam if we have to."

Abu didn't know what to say but reminded himself not to utter anything disrespectful toward the Muslims. *Simply be honest,* he told himself. "We wish no harm on your people," he said. "Only to practice our faith as we please."

The official looked at him and spit. "Get out of here, you dogs," he said, turning and walking away.

At a second checkpoint, ISIS soldiers again detained the family. They called officials at the first checkpoint and were instructed to check the car for valuables. Abu surrendered all he had. When a guard found money that Abu's wife had hidden beneath a seat, he ordered the family out of the car.

"If you convert," said one guard, "all that we took from you will be given back. You will even be protected. So, tell us you embrace Islam."

"I am a Christian," said Abu.

As before, a long round of verbal volleys ensued. Each time the ISIS guard asked Abu to convert, Abu politely but firmly said he was a Christian and would not.

Finally, another guard—a supervisor—came from the booth and fired questions at Abu. *This man*, Abu thought, *is different from the rest, almost like an actor playing a part but deep down not that character himself.*

"So, you have left behind a home and would be willing to pay the tax?" the supervisor asked.

Abu nodded. Yes, the previous checkpoint had taken substantial money that could be used for the tax. And yes, they did own a house. The supervisor instructed the interrogating guard to make a call.

After the guard left, the supervisor turned to Abu. "Begone," he said. "Fast."

Abu felt like a hooked fish fighting for its life, when suddenly the fisherman cut the line. He nodded his thanks and returned to the car.

Upon reaching Erbil, Abu and his family realized the city was already overpopulated with Syrian war refugees. Because of the ISIS purge in Iraq, the city was expanding more each day. What did most of these refugees have in common? They were Christians whose lives had been pulled from underneath them. Students ready to graduate from the University of Mosul now had no records to show they had even been enrolled. Young people engaged to be married didn't know where their fiancées were. Adults who had been employed were now jobless.

They sacrificed it all. They left behind their homes, the lives they had lived, and their hopes for the future, choosing instead to trust in God and serve him wherever he would lead.

The conditions in Erbil were miserable. Nauseating smells rose from garbage and raw sewage. People curled up beneath makeshift tents made of blankets, towels, or scrap materials—anything to protect them from the relentless sun and oppressive heat. They searched desperately for water and food.

Amid all this, Abu set up a lean-to tarp for his family. "Now," he said quietly, "we thank God for a safe journey." And they bowed their heads to pray.

As Abu and his family did, we must remember that the God we serve is with us wherever we go. We must place our hope in him, not in a place or circumstances.

God is far less concerned about where we live than where our hearts are. He cares most about where we place our trust, what we value, and whether the desire of our hearts is to focus our eyes on him. He is pleased when we are so focused on him that we, as the writer of Hebrews did, can affirm our hope and trust with these words: "But as it is, they desire a better country, that is, a heavenly one. Therefore God is not ashamed to be called their God, for he has prepared for them a city" (11:16).

2

JUST ANOTHER DAY

Baris
Turkey

It started as just another workday.

Baris unlocked the front door of the electronics shop he managed, then began tidying up shelves before any customers wandered in.

And that's when he found it: a Bible.

Compelled to pick it up, he decided to read it.

Baris came to the United States from Turkey to complete a master's degree, then stayed when he found work. He and his family—a wife and two children—were living a comfortable life.

Right up until he opened that Bible.

Baris was immediately and deeply touched by Jesus' words in John, chapters 13 through 18. In just a few pages, Jesus answered questions Baris hadn't yet put into words: where Jesus came from, why there were miracles, what followers of Jesus could expect. It was all there.

Like many Muslims drawn to Christ, Baris began experiencing vivid visions. In one, Jesus revealed himself as the Creator God. In another, Baris sensed the depth of Christ's pure, overwhelming love.

So Baris kept reading and studying until he could resist no longer. He embraced Jesus and professed his faith in Christ.

When Baris took his wife aside to tell her he'd become a Christian, her response was immediate—and steely. She demanded a divorce, packed what she'd need to start a new life, and took their sons back to Turkey.

Devastated, Baris didn't want to lose his family, but how could he turn his back on God? Was the sacrifice of his family the cost of following Christ?

He followed his family to Turkey. *If there's any hope of a reconciliation,* he thought, *that's where it will happen.*

He didn't receive the homecoming he'd hoped for. When he told his brother about his conversion, his brother asked Baris to join him at a doctor's office the next day.

Fine, thought Baris, only expecting a half-hour visit. *Maybe I'll even get a chance to share my faith.*

But there was no sharing. Baris was immediately admitted to a psychiatric hospital and medicated with psychotropic drugs. It took weeks for Baris to convince doctors that leaving Islam for Christianity didn't mean he was crazy, and they should release him. Later, his wife would use his stay in the psychiatric hospital as evidence that he was unfit to parent his sons.

Telling his parents about his new faith was equally disastrous. Baris' father exploded in anger, threatening to disown him.

"You can even kill me, and I won't change my mind," Baris replied, after which his mother fainted.

Baris filed for part-time custody of his sons. On the day of one of his court appearances, Baris' former brother-in-law confronted him on a crowded Turkish street, cursing and beating him. "How dare you come here!" he shouted at Baris. "This guy is a missionary, and he cursed Muhammad!" he exclaimed to the many Muslims walking by.

At yet another court appearance, Baris' former father-in-law pushed his way through the courtroom and punched Baris in the face.

Though Baris initially thought about pressing charges to help his custody case, he wasn't at peace about it. He remembered Christ's words in Matthew 5:39: "If they slap you on the right cheek, turn to him the other also."

The court awarded Baris visitation rights, but his ex-wife often changes plans or skips visits. She seems determined to poison Baris' relationship with his sons.

Still, he has his faith in Christ…and purpose.

Baris serves the Lord by connecting local Christians with Turks who are searching for truth. He and his team distribute Bibles, and Baris visits new believers and people who have questions about Christianity.

Some of Baris' work happens through the internet. This allows him to connect with isolated believers and provides an opportunity for Baris to share his faith. Live chats are especially effective—in one six-month period, forty people placed their faith in Christ.

Baris longs to see a church in every Turkish city, so when new believers face the consequences of that decision, they won't be alone. He knows the painful challenges of loneliness and loss, and the healing power of having a family in Christ. "When they are alone, it is really hard to remain in the faith," Baris said.

He also knows Turkey's cultural allegiance to Islamic values plus every political shift ramp up the challenges faced by believers.

But in spite of the danger and sacrifice, Baris persists.

Every day he rises with hope. Hope he can lead one more person to Jesus…and hope he'll one day hug his sons again.

We're often reminded of the sacrifices made by people in the Bible for the sake of the gospel. Stephen's stoning. Paul's beatings and imprisonment. John the Baptist's beheading.

But those who lived and suffered for Christ in ancient times aren't alone. There are believers in the world today being killed, imprisoned, and beheaded.

And losing their families.

Pray for Baris and all our brothers and sisters who daily offer sacrifices in obedience to God's Word as biblical disciples. Lift them up asking God to give them strength, passion, and—even in the midst of their sacrifice—joy.

3

HOPE FROM ON HIGH

Hussein
Iran

By age seventeen, Hussein was a full-fledged drug addict trapped in a prison of his own choices. He was hungry for something more, even though he didn't know what. But he happened upon it while channel surfing one day. A particular television show stood out above the rest. Transmitted by satellite far above Iran, it carried the gospel message straight into Hussein's home.

That day, Hussein heard the message that Jesus died for his sins and wanted a relationship with him. He began to understand that Jesus was about love, grace, and hope, not rules and regulations. This message of compassion created a deep struggle within him.

One part of him related to these statements: *I'm a drug dealer. Drug dealers are bad. So I'm bad. Surely God hates me.*

Yet the man on the television had said the opposite: "God loves you right where you are, whether you are a world ambassador or a drug addict. You matter to him. And he wants you to live the fullest life possible for him."

Those words, and the simple gospel message, penetrated Hussein's hardened heart and mind. He committed his life to Jesus that day, and his life turned from hopeless to hopeful, from lost to saved, from death to life. His desire for drugs faded. His love for other people grew stronger.

Some people weren't happy about Hussein's conversion and wanted to kill him, snuffing out any impact of his Christian witness. His Muslim father turned on Hussein, reporting him to authorities in hopes his "apostate" son would be arrested. His father's response actually understated how much he despised Hussein's decision to follow Jesus.

"I hope they decide to hang you [for apostasy]," his father spat. "If they do, I will be the one who'll put the rope around your neck."

The new believer was indeed arrested. To honor Hussein's father for his military service during the Iran-Iraq War, the judge chose not to execute Hussein. Instead, he was thrown into a prison where guards were free to carry out their own form of justice.

Hussein wanted to stand for Jesus; they broke one of his legs.

Hussein wanted to praise God with music; they broke all his fingers.

Hussein wanted to bow before Christ in humility; they ripped open his back with forty lashes from a whip.

Yet, during Hussein's time in prison, his love did grow. With each sacrifice required of him—his leg, his hands, his back, his future—he continued to honor God and share his faith.

His love for Jesus and willingness to forgive spoke most loudly when he shared the gospel with the prison guard in charge of his torture. Deeply touched, the guard gave Hussein his card and asked the teenager to contact him later so he could learn more.

Then Hussein was released.

His high school expelled him, giving him no chance to further his education or attend a university. All his academic records were deleted, as if telling the world, *this person never existed.*

But despite his suffering, Hussein later wrote, "None of these punishments made me upset, except that I cannot play music for the Lord now."

Hussein not only existed, but his time of painful persecution tested his faith and actually taught him to live more fully for God. Rather than relying on human relationships to sustain him, Hussein placed his ultimate hope in God, who through John communicated these words: "Do not be surprised, brothers, that the world hates you" (1 John 3:13).

Hussein, who simply responded to the message of hope featured on a television broadcast, learned quickly that God wants his people to make him their highest priority, knowing that our love for him will, in turn, fuel our love for others.

What an impact we too can have when we rely on God and his Spirit to help us endure sacrifices brought about by our faith and express Christ-centered, compassionate love to those around us! Ask God to help you rely on his Spirit today to embrace whatever sacrifices of faith he calls you to endure as his witness.

4

RISING ABOVE THE FAMILY BEATINGS

Nadia and Rachel
Pakistan

Whenever eleven-year-old Nadia walked by the neighborhood church, her parents' words of warning jolted her from curiosity. "Nadia, you are to ignore the infidels and their church. It is an affront to your Muslim faith."

She would tug on her colorful headscarf as she walked hurriedly past the church. But the building, the cross that towered above it, the people inside, and the God she could overhear them talking about piqued her interest.

"Jesus," she heard a man say over the church loudspeaker, "is the way, the truth, and the life." Nadia did not know what these words meant, yet they intrigued her. *If Jesus is the way,* she wondered, *then why am I a Muslim?* Those words proved to be spiritual seeds planted in the deep, rich soil of her soul, and they would bear fruit.

In time, Nadia became friends with a girl about her age, Rachel, who attended the church and lived nearby. This gave Nadia the opportunity to inundate Rachel with questions she had stored up during the years.

"Who is this Jesus you speak of?" Nadia asked.

"He is God-become-man, the maker of all."

"Even me?"

"Yes, Nadia, even you," Rachel replied. "And me. And everyone. He loves us and desires a relationship with us."

"What does he *expect* of us?" Nadia continued. "What must we do to be in his kingdom? What rules must we keep? What rituals must we perform?"

Rachel touched her friend's hand while lightly shaking her head. "It is not like that. He doesn't want your rituals or your rules. He wants your heart. Your trust. With that, you will *want* to obey."

What kind of God is this? Nadia mused.

After Rachel gave her a Bible, Nadia discreetly started reading it and began to understand. This was a God of grace. Of love. Of compassion. He even knew the exact number of hairs on her head and would leave ninety-nine sheep to save one—perhaps her. This God was quite unlike the one she was raised to believe in, and she desired to be part of his kingdom.

Soon Nadia placed her trust in Christ, a secret she shared only with Rachel. But when Nadia's brother, Miled, discovered her praying and going to church, he flew into a rage. He began beating her weekly.

He insisted that she deny Christ. She refused.

He followed her to church one morning, caught up with her, grabbed her by the back of the neck, took her home, and beat her black and blue.

"How dare you enter that church!" he exclaimed. "Have you forgotten that you are a Muslim? You're never to set foot in that church again!"

"I should be free to attend church," she protested.

He picked up a wooden bowl and slammed it into her forehead, splitting the skin above her eye. As blood poured out, he shoved her into her bedroom and locked the door. He kept her there for weeks, entering only to give her small amounts of food and water along with many welts and bruises. Not one of her other family members objected to his brutality or tried to help her.

Finally, she escaped and found refuge with a pastor and his family. Because Nadia was a former Muslim, however, her presence put others at risk. Fearing retaliation, the pastor soon asked her to find someplace else to live.

When she wanted to be baptized, three pastors turned her down because they feared they would be attacked, or their churches would be burned. Eventually, a pastor in a distant town agreed to baptize Nadia. She felt a happiness she had never known before.

God then blessed her with a Christian man, whom she later married. But when her parents learned of the marriage, they registered kidnapping complaints against the man. They claimed he had lured her away from her Muslim faith. Miled found the couple and beat Nadia's husband so badly his eardrum ruptured.

Because the couple had to go into hiding, Nadia's husband could not find work. Other Christians, however, helped him start his own business where he could still keep a low profile.

Beatings. Ostracizing. False accusations. Nadia and her husband made the sacrifices and endured the abuse in order to cling to their faith in Christ.

During a time of prayer with another Christian, Nadia did not mention her own needs. She said only this: "Oh, Jesus, Son of God, you know me very well. You saved my husband's life when my brother attacked him and beat him badly. When we were hungry, you provided meals and a place to live. Jesus, we trust that you will never leave us. Amen."

Amen indeed.

Nadia's hope rests in the confidence that Jesus will never leave us. His great, sacrificial love inspires us to treat others as he has treated us. "'For I was hungry and you gave me food, I was thirsty and you gave me drink, I was a stranger and you welcomed me, I was naked and you clothed me, I was sick and you visited me, I was in prison and you came to me.'...And the King will answer them, 'Truly, I say to you, as you did it to one of the least of these my brothers, you did it to me'" (Matthew 25:35–36, 40).

What a privilege we have to thank God for taking care of us by being his hands and feet to care for others—whether they live next door or in a faraway country. May we pray for God's guidance in discovering others' needs and learn to be more sensitive to the Holy Spirit's leading in caring for them.

5

HIS OLD FRIEND LUKE

Nemrut
Iraq

Seventeen-year-old Nemrut loved books—all books. But in his dusty Iraqi town, few Kurdish-language books were available.

Then one day he spotted something new in a neighborhood bookstore: a Kurdish translation of the Gospel of Luke. Nemrut had no idea what it was, but he knew he hadn't yet read it.

When he handed the book to the shop owner, Nemrut was disappointed to discover it wasn't for sale. It was the owner's only copy, so he was reluctant to let it go.

Nemrut negotiated with the owner, offering to pay a lending fee and bring the book back when he was finished.

Done.

After Nemrut carefully carried the book home, he began to read it. He read and read until four o'clock the next morning.

Nemrut returned the book as promised but couldn't put it out of his mind. It had stirred something inside him.

Like many Kurdish Muslims, Nemrut wasn't especially committed to Islam. He held his faith lightly, more loyal to family and tribe than to religion. But when he joined one of Kurdistan's largest political parties, he knew he had best get serious about Islam.

And Nemrut's solution was to read the Quran…three times.

Try as he might, he couldn't get comfortable with what he found there, especially the instructions to hate and kill others.

Since he was known as an avid reader, Nemrut was put in charge of his political party's bookstore. As soon as he could, he purchased a New Testament to add to the store's collection.

Nemrut sped through the book in less than a month, taking notes as he turned the pages. *This is my old friend, Luke,* he thought when he reached Luke's Gospel.

When he finished, Nemrut totaled up how often the New Testament spoke about love: 345 times.

And not once did it urge readers to hate or kill others.

Nemrut decided to devote his life to Jesus and his teachings. But as a Muslim, the teenager had no idea that he could become a Christian. In the next three years, he read through the New Testament three more times.

Nemrut also loaned the store's copy to others, but he had first written instructions on the cover: "Read this carefully and intentionally. Keep it in purity, and then return it to me."

When Nemrut finally met an actual Christian—a man distributing Bibles in his city—Nemrut quietly took the man aside to ask a question that had burned in him for years. "Can anyone become a Christian? I have read the Bible, I know the Bible, but I don't know if I can become a Christian."

Nemrut learned he had become a Christian the moment he put his faith in Jesus Christ and turned from the teachings of Islam.

Rejoicing, Nemrut continued telling friends about Jesus, and many placed their trust in Christ. The group of believers grew to twenty and met in Nemrut's home, which came to the attention of a local mullah.

The next Friday, the mullah made an announcement to everyone attending mosque.

"Some people became Christians in our town because of Nemrut," the mullah said angrily. "Anyone who will drink with them will become an infidel. If you drink water from his house, you become an infidel. You shouldn't speak to them, you shouldn't greet them, and you should cut off relations with them because they became infidels."

Persecution began in earnest right away.

Nemrut and his small group were beaten and cursed. Lifelong friendships were severed. Nemrut's sister built a fence between their adjoining properties; he and his wife no longer had access to a bathroom they had shared. His wife, who had yet to fully place her trust in Christ, was frightened and constantly cried.

One Friday, after morning prayers, police intercepted a mob of nearly two hundred men marching toward Nemrut's house. The head of security warned Nemrut that next time he wouldn't be able to stop the attackers.

"Why don't you stop reading the Bible and speaking to people?" he asked.

After he publicly embraced Christ, Nemrut felt he could no longer remain in the Kurdish political party and thus lost his job. Needing to scratch together a living, he became a freelance trader, ferrying goods in and out of a city on the Iraq-Iran border. But his new "career" would lead him to his next endeavor.

As one who carried goods back and forth across the border, Nemrut knew the Iranian government forbade three things from entering the country: weapons, drugs, and Bibles. Nemrut refused to traffic in the first two, but Bibles? The Bible had changed his life so dramatically he wanted everyone to have one.

One day Nemrut bought all thirty-five Farsi Bibles at a Bible society. He boldly wrote his name and phone number inside each before smuggling them into Iran. It was risky, but Nemrut was prepared to sacrifice whatever it took to make Bibles available. If he was discovered, he'd deal with the consequences. Until then, he'd keep working.

When Iranians who received Bibles contacted Nemrut, he quietly met with them in his border city. He taught them what he could about Jesus Christ, then sent them back to Iran to share the gospel.

Nemrut was honest about what the new evangelists might encounter. He told them if they were beaten, it was no worse than what Christ also suffered.

Others heard of Nemrut's work and provided him with more Farsi Bibles. Over the course of ten years, Nemrut sent nearly 310,000 Bibles into Iran before Iranian government surveillance forced him to stop.

The 2014 ISIS invasion of Mosul made Kurdistan even more dangerous for Christians. Strangers appeared in Nemrut's yard, terrorizing his family. Death threats were a regular occurrence.

Deeply troubled, Nemrut and his wife prayed. "You cannot force them to accept Jesus," his wife told him, suggesting they should leave. Though Nemrut agreed with his wife, the couple continued to pray and by morning realized they needed to stay.

But…how?

That's when a Kurdish church in Erbil called, asking if Nemrut would serve as their pastor. The move would keep him in Iraq but move his family out of the spotlight in their small village. He pastored the church for three years.

Nemrut still has a vision to reach his people, the Kurds, with the gospel. And he will keep telling others the story of Jesus, whom he first encountered in a borrowed book about his old friend Luke.

Nemrut's decision to follow Christ came at a cost. First, he lost his livelihood. Then, he gave up physical security to obey Christ by remaining in Kurdistan, knowing the risk involved.

Obedience to Christ will be costly for you, too. Jesus predicted suffering would mark the lives of those who follow him. But he also promised to be with his followers in their pain, and that persecution could refine their faith—and their purpose, which is in alignment with God's.

Have you counted the cost of following Jesus? Are you prepared to suffer as you grow in obedience to Christ and his Great Commission?

6

TRIUMPHANT IN DEATH

Abdiwelli
Kenya

Growing up in Garissa, Kenya, Abdiwelli Ahmed (Abdi) was wholly committed to Islam. He even led his high school's Islamic society.

But while a college student, Abdi began questioning Islam. *Is Islam the only way to get to heaven?*

A dangerous thought for a young Muslim.

Abdi's questioning continued. *Where will I end up in the afterlife? And how can I know the answer to that question now?*

"Muhammad himself said he didn't know if he would go to hell or heaven, and he didn't know the fate of the people who followed him," Abdi said. He realized Muhammad led without certainty, and Abdi refused to follow a blind guide.

Abdi found a Bible and quietly read it whenever he was alone. The account of Creation in Genesis opened his eyes to God's majestic power, and he discovered God's tender love in 1 Corinthians, chapter 13. Jesus' farewell to his followers in John, chapter 14, moved Abdi to tears—and closer to faith in Christ.

After soul-searching discussions with a Christian friend, Abdi was ready: he placed his faith in Christ and finally experienced the peace and eternal security he'd long desired.

But when other students and faculty at Abdi's college learned he'd left Islam, they responded with violence. They considered Christian converts a danger to their religion. From that moment on, Abdi was a marked man. He was beaten up. His life was in danger.

One day Abdi was hit in the head with a stone, causing severe bleeding. He hid in his mother's house but, when he saw a mob approaching, he ran again—this time to a friend's home. He knew people were eager to kill him.

It's like they're a cat and I'm a mouse, he thought. *I'm being hunted in my own hometown.*

Abdi quickly fled to seek guidance from a relative, Pastor Ibrahim, who planted churches and shared the gospel with Somali Muslims in northern Kenya. Ibrahim took Abdi to a campus ministry center where Abdi was introduced to other believers, including a young woman named Helen.

When Helen met Abdi, she was drawn to his contagious faith and commitment. "I love the Lord, and I'm ready to die for Christ," he told her.

The two eventually married, launching into ministry almost immediately. For three years they lived in Niger, working with the Tuareg tribe. They then ministered in Addis Ababa, finally joining a Somali-focused ministry that sent them to a Kenyan village near the Somali border. At the time, the village was nearly 90 percent Somali.

Abdi and Helen served Somalis through an agriculture-development ministry. They built relationships and, when opportunities arose, shared the gospel.

Right away they were met with stiff resistance from local Muslims. One night a mob appeared at the couple's house with containers of gasoline.

They want to burn the house down, Abdi realized. *Now what will we do?*

A local government official who witnessed the incident quickly drove the couple to a police station where they'd be safe from attack—at least for the moment.

And when death threats continued, the husband and wife prayed together, finding peace in the assurance God was with them.

For a while, the boiling anger directed toward Abdi and Helen calmed to a simmer.

As the two began feeling safer, they opened their home to a few believers for Bible study.

Clearly, Abdi wasn't backing down or stepping away from his ministry. "Our desire is to know God and to make him known, so many Somalis can become Christians, be discipled, and return back to their homes," he said. Abdi even began visiting neighboring countries, sharing the gospel with Somali expatriates.

In Somalia, it's illegal to convert from Islam or to share the gospel. Christians are actively targeted by the terrorist group al-Shabab as well as by family members. Christians are often pursued by hostile Somalis even after leaving the country.

Abdi was one such Christian.

On February 7, 2013, twenty years after Abdi placed his faith in Christ, three assassins shot him to death as he talked with a pastor in the center of town.

Grieving and in shock, Helen and her three sons left Garissa and returned to her home country of Nigeria. God drew her and the boys closer to him. And in time they found hope and encouragement to share with a hurting world lost in sin.

Helen and her sons visited Garissa on June 21, 2020. She was surprised to learn her martyred husband had gained a certain fame and was told that "every Somali knows his witness."

Abdi's influence continues in many East African Somali communities and even extends to Europe and the United States. Countless lives have been touched by his testimony, and countless more by his faithful sacrifice.

Abdi's sons know their father is in heaven, and they see God using their father's death to advance his purposes. Helen remains committed to following Christ and serving Somali Muslims, just as her husband did. His sacrifice—and hers—haven't dimmed her passion for Christ.

When friends warn her to be careful lest she also find herself killed for the gospel, Helen responds boldly: "If I try saving my life, I will lose it.

"We have a triumphant God," she says, eyes shining. "We know he is going to triumph in this situation."

Abdi's sacrifice was great, and the grief that Helen and her sons have experienced is real and deep. But his sacrifice was not unexpected. He knew what proclaiming Christ might cost, but he and Helen didn't abandon sharing the gospel to protect earthly lives they'd eventually lose anyway.

Instead, they kept their eyes fixed on eternity: pleasing Christ and gaining a life that can't be taken away…ever.

The apostle Paul cautioned the church at Corinth not to look at the things that are seen but those that are unseen, because what we experience here and now on this earth is what Paul called a "light momentary affliction." And that affliction is preparing "for us an eternal weight of glory beyond all comparison" (2 Corinthians 4:17–18).

Beyond all comparison. Think about that!

As you view your life through the lens of eternity, the things that are unseen, what are you willing to sacrifice to advance Christ's eternal purposes? What price is too great to pay?

7

A "FOOL" FOR CHRIST

Kazim
Pakistan

After eight days of being forced to chop wood from sunrise to sunset, Kazim hardly recognized the axe. Once ash white, its handle was now red from his bleeding hands.

"Now will you cast aside this Christ love?" asked Mohammed Shafiq, a village elder. "Now will you come to your senses?"

Kazim was bent over, exhausted, thinking of his wife, Yasmeen. Sweat dripped from the tip of his nose. His clothes reeked. He shook his head and exclaimed, "No. Never."

"You are a fool," said Shafiq, raising his beating stick high as if he, too, were chopping wood. His face reflected a blend of satisfaction and frustration. With an audible *oomph*, he slammed the stick across Kazim's blistered back.

"Ahhh!" Kazim yelled, grimacing and trying to find the will to withstand yet another blow.

"Quit loafing," the elder said. "We need more wood." Then he swiftly kicked Kazim into the dirt.

Before this persecution began, Kazim farmed by day and evangelized by night. After one of his twelve-hour days, he bicycled home to share a quick meal of chapati and rice with Yasmeen.

"You are wearing yourself thin," she said to him. "You cannot do it all."

He looked at her—the woman whose smile still melted his heart. "The sooner I spread God's Word, the sooner I am back with you," he answered and teasingly took hold of her shawl and pulled her close.

Another day, while Kazim bicycled to the market, Shafiq forced him to stop. "We know you have prayed in the name of Jesus," he said. "Our prophet, Muhammad, is a true prophet. Your prophet is a liar."

"Jesus Christ is the true and living God," Kazim replied. "I worship him and preach his message to other people."

"Is this true?" the elder asked, his eyes squinting. Nodding his head slightly in mock threat, he continued, "Well, let's see what other people think of your worshiping and preaching this Jesus dung."

Shafiq turned to the crowds scurrying from vendor to vendor. "Did you hear this, my friends?" he shouted above the din. "This man—this lower-than-a-snake man—boasts that he bows before Jesus and gloats in telling others of this false God."

Like angry bees, passersby descended on Kazim. Joined by Shafiq, they dragged him away. That's when they forced him to chop wood until he would recant his faith in Christ. When he did not recant, they let him go.

But one night as Kazim prepared for his nightly ministry, Shafiq and five other militant Muslims confronted him again. Kazim beckoned his seven-year-old nephew, Rachid, to come to him. He turned to the boy.

"Today they will kill me," he whispered. "Please take my Bible and keep it with you." He then gently pushed the boy away, as if his nephew were a little boat and Kazim were sending him off to sea.

When Kazim turned his head, Shafiq brandished a semiautomatic pistol and anxiously fingered its trigger. He pointed it at Kazim's head. "Today I will shoot you if you do not accept the prophet Muhammad as the one and only true prophet."

Kazim looked intently into Shafiq's eyes. "I cannot do this. If you want to shoot me, do it. I will happily accept being killed. But remember; if this is not God's will, you cannot kill me."

Shafiq kept the pistol pointed at Kazim's head for several minutes. Then his hand began to shake. He pulled out his cell phone and reported to the police that Kazim had tried to rob him.

Later, after Kazim arrived at the police station, officers initiated a new round of torture that lasted for thirteen days. They tied his hands behind his back. They beat the bottoms of his feet.

They yanked on his beard, and one officer said, "The prophet Muhammad had a beard, and you dare compare our prophet to Jesus!" They dragged him across the dirt floor. Mocked him. Spit on him.

Sometimes they stripped off his clothes and lashed his back and buttocks with a leather strap.

"This can all stop when you accept Islam," one man said.

"No."

The officer slapped him across the face, and Kazim shook his head no.

Finally, the police officers registered the false robbery charges against him and sent him to a district jail. Pain radiated through his shoulders and across his back. Weak and too exhausted to speak, Kazim still felt a peace he could barely comprehend, especially when he held a tattered Bible that a fellow prisoner had given him. His lone frustration? His eyes were too swollen to read that Bible; so the inmate who'd given it to him read to him every day.

Four months after Kazim's arrest, he was released on bail. When he returned home, Yasmeen was gone. Shafiq, his tormentor, had moved in and was using their possessions, claiming their livestock as his own, and reveling in his "ownership" of his new property.

"If you don't leave immediately," he ordered Kazim, "I will shoot you and your wife, when we find her."

With only two dollars to his name, Kazim found Yasmeen in the village. They fled, leaving everything behind. The couple stopped for help at various friends' homes, but their friends kept turning them away, fearing they, too, would be targets for persecution.

Kazim and Yasmeen rushed to another village, where a Christian man allowed them to stay in a small building he owned.

He also provided them with clothing, food, and a Bible. "I knew that God would provide help," Kazim said, "but I didn't know how he would do it. I had one blessing with me—the freedom to preach the Word." Other Christians who learned of the couple's plight purchased a rickshaw for Kazim so he could support his family as a taxi driver.

Some people would call Kazim a fool. The scars on his back may never fade away. He may never reclaim his home. He may always have nightmares about his beatings.

But Kazim is the kind of fool the apostle Paul wrote about: "We are fools for Christ's sake, but you are wise in Christ. We are weak, but you are strong. You are held in honor, but we in disrepute. To the present hour we hunger and thirst, we are poorly dressed and buffeted and homeless, and we labor, working with our own hands. When reviled, we bless; when persecuted, we endure; when slandered, we entreat. We have become, and are still, like the scum of the world, the refuse of all things" (1 Corinthians 4:10–13).

No amount of earthly humiliation or pain can demoralize people who have made the choice to give their lives for Christ's sake. We may be weak in ourselves, yet we are strong in him. "We forget all our worries," Kazim said, "and even today we still feel fresh in Jesus' faith. I start each day in prayer and then drive my rickshaw."

May each of us, like Kazim, give away our lives for Christ's sake daily.

8

NOTHING TO LOSE

Khaled
Yemen

After leading prayer at his mosque in Yemen, Khaled sat in a café. But instead of the usual buzz of conversation, patrons were riveted on the shop's television.

An endless loop of planes slamming into tall towers played over and over on the screen, cutting away to show terrified crowds rushing through New York City's streets, engulfed by massive clouds of dust and debris.

To Khaled, it looked like hell on earth. Yet, all around him, fellow Muslims were cheering and clapping one another on the back.

Khaled was shocked at their reaction.

Three thousand people were killed, he thought. *What kind of religion is that?*

On September 11, 2001, the Twin Towers weren't all that collapsed.

Khaled's Muslim faith crumbled as well. When he walked out of the café, Khaled also walked away from Islam.

Growing up, Khaled was taught that Christians were morally inferior. However, when he realized the Quran validated his father's abuse of his mother, he became angry and questioned Islam. He was conflicted. He knew criticizing his father's actions was criticizing Islam.

His father's death provided Khaled with the opportunity to walk away from Islam; he turned to the Yemeni Socialist Party. But it was the year he married Samira that he learned more about Jesus through an unlikely source. While reading a socialist newspaper, Khaled found something unusual: a reference to the words of Jesus in John 8:7: "Let him who is without sin among you be the first to throw a stone at her."

The description of Jesus' gracious encounter with a woman stunned Khaled. It didn't sound like the Jesus described in the Quran. His misconceptions about Christianity were shattered.

As he supported his family by teaching Islamic studies and Arabic at a high school, he couldn't stop thinking about Christ's words in John 8:7.

And he would once again encounter Christ's words.

Later that year, Samira's uncle gave Khaled some books he no longer wanted. One of those books included a Gospel of Matthew. Khaled devoured it and discussed Christ's teachings with his students, hoping he'd find a copy of the full Bible.

When one of his students told Khaled about a Christian radio broadcast, he found an old radio and hauled it up to his roof where he could listen in private.

There on the rooftop, every night at ten thirty, he sat under the stars and trembled with excitement as he heard about Christ's love and forgiveness. Hearing those hopeful words in his own Yemeni dialect assured him there were others among his people considering Christianity. He knew the risks involved in leaving Islam—especially for a religion like Christianity.

In Yemen, converting from Islam to Christianity is a crime punishable by death. For Muslim families, becoming a Christian is shameful. The church in Yemen is essentially invisible, with only a few thousand believers.

The more Khaled listened, the more questions he had.

He texted his questions to the program's host; weeks later, he prayed with one of the hosts over the phone and placed his faith in Jesus Christ.

Khaled was now counted among the small number of Christians in his country.

The next morning, Khaled felt like a new man, but he kept his conversion secret—even from his wife.

He knew he needed fellowship with other believers, regardless of the danger. When he discovered a few lived in a nearby town, he began meeting them there for Bible study.

But Khaled's frequent absences worried Samira. What was he doing? Why was he so secretive? What was he hiding?

Concerned her husband had found a new wife, she eventually confronted him.

"I love you," Khaled assured her with tears, "but I have become a Christian."

"Are you an infidel?" she asked him.

"No," he replied. "But I love Jesus." He then told her how Jesus changed his life.

Samira had noticed a difference, but she didn't know what had inspired those changes.

After learning the truth, Samira also gave her life to Christ. Together, the husband and wife embarked on a journey of growth and discipleship, which led to the couple declaring their faith through baptism.

But Samira's decision cost her everything.

Somehow, the Muslim Brotherhood obtained photos of Samira's baptism. They posted those pictures on a social media site that targeted evangelists in Yemen. Days later, DVDs—including the family's address and the address of Khaled's school—were distributed in their community. Khaled was called "The Big Evangelist" on the DVD.

And that's when the persecution began.

Khaled was mocked and assaulted by teachers at his school. His car windows were smashed, and tires slashed. Someone even poisoned his dog and her three puppies. And Samira was attacked in the streets by Khaled's twenty-two-year-old nephew. The couple's children were emotionally and verbally abused at school.

Then early one morning, Khaled woke up to his son's screams. "Mother is on fire in the kitchen!"

Someone had poured gasoline into Samira's jar of cooking oil. It ignited, engulfing her in flames. A neighbor reported seeing a person enter the house several days earlier; Khaled suspects it was a relative.

Once it was known she was a Christian, Samira's care at the hospital all but disappeared. Nurses quit changing bandages on her extensive, third-degree burns. Khaled was forced to find and pay for her medicine himself. The attending physician eventually prescribed new medication—but it contained a compound that likely claimed Samira's life.

She died at age thirty-three.

Before she passed, Samira whispered to Khaled that she forgave those who had persecuted their family, including the individual responsible for her burns.

Khaled found it difficult to match Samira's Christ-like grace, but eventually he, too, forgave those who persecuted his family—and murdered his wife. He even made his forgiveness public, writing: "Everyone who persecuted me verbally, with their actions, by encouraging others to persecute me—any way directly or indirectly—I forgive you."

His family's sacrifices have given Khaled an eternal perspective, one that looks past their losses to a glorious future. God continues to use their pain for his purposes. For example, his brother-in-law, who once angrily debated religion with Khaled online, recently finished a discussion by saying, "May the Lord Jesus Christ bless you." Moments like this encourage Khaled to continue sharing the gospel despite his broken heart.

"Praise the Lord for what happened," Khaled said, "because right now I have nothing to lose."

Khaled's decision to follow Christ cost him his wife and his homeland, knowing he and his children were likely next. He didn't choose to see his beloved Samira suffer and die because she loved God. Yet Khaled doesn't blame God for the actions of the unknown intruder who killed his wife. Instead, he trusts God and offers the murderer the same forgiveness he's received himself.

Like Job, he is not charging God with wrong. Job said, "Naked I came from my mother's womb, and naked shall I return. The Lord gave, and the Lord has taken away; blessed be the name of the Lord." In all this, Job did not sin or charge God with wrong.

Each day, Khaled sets aside a desire to blame God and to settle the score of an injustice that ripped open his life.

Khaled is sacrificing vengeance in his flesh and choosing forgiveness.

QUESTIONS FOR REFLECTION AND DISCUSSION

SACRIFICE

1. How would you define the word "sacrifice?" How would you explain to a new Christian the sacrificial choices biblical disciples make? What story in this section assists your explanation? How does the story bring clarity about the sacrifices Christians make in order to fully follow Christ?

2. Read Philippians 2:5–11, an early hymn of the church. As you read, note each of the sacrifices Christ made in order to bring redemption to humanity:

    "Have this mind among yourselves, which is yours in Christ Jesus" (verse 5)

    a. verse 6
    b. verse 7
    c. verse 8

    i.   Read verse 8 again. Which two characteristics did Christ model that give biblical disciples the ability to sacrifice? Why do you think these characteristics were important for Christ to be able to sacrifice all that he did?

    ii.   In verses 9–11, what is the result of Christ's sacrifice?

d.   Reflect on the difficult sacrifice Baris made in order to live boldly for Christ. How did Baris display humility? How did he live in obedience to God? What role does embracing humility play in our ability to sacrifice? How is obedience to God demonstrated in our sacrificial choices?

e.   Can you think of something you have willingly sacrificed in order to live for Christ? What was it? Did you sacrifice joyfully? Why or why not?

3.   Think through Abdiwelli's story of sacrifice. At every turn in his spiritual journey, Abdi experienced harassment, threats, violence, and finally death. How do you think each experience of persecution prepared him to be obedient to God? Can you think of a specific part of his story as an example?

4.   Some of our Christian brothers and sisters in this section gave the ultimate sacrifice for their faith in Christ.

a.   Read Revelation 12:11. What does the phrase "for they loved not their lives even unto death" mean? How does this describe those we read about in this section? How might loving one's life prevent sacrificial living?

b. What attitudes and actions do you possess that indicate you love Christ more than your own life?

Pray

Ask God for the willingness to sacrifice for the sake of Christ and to count it joy. Pray for our persecuted Christian family—who sacrifice greatly for the activities of their faith at the hands of Islamic extremists—that their sacrifices advance the gospel.

Part II

COURAGE

Be sober-minded; be watchful. Your adversary the devil prowls around like a roaring lion, seeking someone to devour. Resist him, firm in your faith, knowing that the same kinds of suffering are being experienced by your brotherhood throughout the world. And after you have suffered a little while, the God of all grace, who has called you to his eternal glory in Christ, will himself restore, confirm, strengthen, and establish you.

1 Peter 5:8–10

When we live among people who are resistant to or openly hostile toward the gospel, it is hard—sometimes terrifying—to stand strong and live as Christ's witnesses. But since the earliest Bible times, God has called people to serve him as they faced challenging circumstances. God knows the threats and dangers that lie ahead, and he has a message for those who will serve him faithfully. After Moses died, Joshua faced an uphill battle in leading the ancient

Israelites to fight and possess the Promised Land. God said to him, "Have I not commanded you? Be strong and courageous. Do not be frightened, and do not be dismayed, for the LORD your God is with you wherever you go" (Joshua 1:9).

David, who faced many frightening challenges and overcame great difficulties, shared God's sustaining message in Psalm 27:14: "Wait for the LORD; be strong, and let your heart take courage; wait for the LORD!"

Having courage to move forward in obedience, despite obvious perils, is not based on human emotion or acting because of an adrenaline rush. Courage to stand for Jesus does not come from assessing the risks and strategically balancing benefits against losses. Courage comes from knowing the risks and moving forward anyway. If we want to stand for Christ, we cannot let fear paralyze our hearts and cause us to disobey.

Human courage will fail the follower of Christ who shares the gospel in a neighborhood where Islamic militants are in control. Human courage is insufficient to motivate a pastor and his wife to remain in territory controlled by Islamic extremists where they hold clandestine Bible studies to help new believers grow in understanding and commitment to Christ. Facing persecution for our faith is rooted in the knowledge that God is at work in and through us to accomplish his will. This courage, a biblical courage, shows itself even in the midst of violent, life-threatening situations.

Such courage is nurtured by our trust in God's power and strength to stand against insurmountable odds. It draws confidence from the example and promise of Christ: "When they deliver you over, do not be anxious how you are to speak or what you are to say, for what you are to say will be given to you in that hour. ... And whoever does not take his cross and follow me is not worthy of me" (Matthew 10:19, 38).

Such courage matures through our ongoing commitment to view circumstances in light of God's eternal perspective and to rely on God alone for strength to endure. Such courage leads to bold action despite all risks.

We live in a world in which even small acts that suggest allegiance to Jesus Christ—asking foreign visitors for a Bible, not responding to the Muslim call to prayer, asking questions of a known Christian—can trigger horrible retribution. Therefore, courage that is rooted in God's power and faithfulness is essential.

The following stories show Spirit-empowered courage at work in the lives of those who bear the mark "I am n" and gratefully trust God to provide for them moment by moment.

9

THE THEOLOGY OF PAIN

Naasir and Hoda
Egypt

A low haze of pollution hung over the sprawling city of Cairo, made even more pungent by cigarette smoke and vehicle exhaust. Amid the hustle and bustle, horns honked. Pushy hawkers preyed on tourists who had come to see the ancient tombs, ornate mosques, and the Giza pyramids that rise majestically on the western edge of the city.

But Naasir and Hoda were not tourists. The young married couple were headed to a housing complex, thankful to have found a place to live—even if it was in a rundown apartment building.

As they passed a group of men, one of them spat at Hoda's feet. He mumbled something about her not having her head covered. Hoda understood his scorn. Most Muslim women cover their heads, most Christian women do not.

The landlord, an older woman, welcomed the thirty-something couple and their nine-year-old son, but she looked skeptically at Hoda. Nevertheless, she told them about the apartment and explained the price and terms. Then she asked a few questions about their rental history, income, and other details.

"Well?" Naasir asked. "Can we have it?"

The woman looked unsure, as if something were bothering her. She glanced quickly at Hoda, and then looked away. "Yes," she said with a hint of reluctance. "It is yours if you want it."

"Oh, thank you, thank you," said Naasir.

"We are grateful to you," Hoda added.

Finding a place to live had been difficult. Twelve times landlords had kicked the couple out of their apartments after learning they were Christians. Yet Naasir and Hoda remained firm in their commitment to be honest if anyone asked if they were Muslims. Once they had been—but not anymore.

Their relief was short-lived, however. As they were leaving, the woman's husband appeared. He looked directly at Hoda and then at his wife.

"You told them, of course," he stated, "that the apartment has already gone to someone else, right?"

"I told them they could have it," she replied.

"What?" he exclaimed and then turned to Hoda. "Where is your hijab?"

Hoda glanced at Naasir, then answered, "I am…a Christian."

"Then you do not get the apartment!" the man declared.

"I saw her lack of covering," his wife said, "but we need the money. The place has been empty for six months."

"And we have an agreement," Naasir said hopefully.

"You have nothing!" the man responded. "Nothing but disrespect for Islam. Leave. Now!"

"This is not fair," Naasir pleaded. "Just because we don't agree—"

"Leave!" the man repeated. "There are millions of people in Cairo. There are thousands of judges. Not one will side with you."

"Come," said Hoda, "we must go."

In Egypt, the "iron furnace" has grown even hotter for Christ-followers. Radical Islamic theology has rooted itself deeper into society. Muslim extremists have infiltrated government departments. The country's constitution now states that sharia (Islamic) law must be the basis for all legislation. Attacks against Coptic Orthodox Christians, whose ancestors embraced Christianity during the first centuries after Christ, have increased. But Christian converts from Islam suffer the most, Naasir and Hoda among them. Despite such discrimination, the two cling courageously to their faith.

Hoda came to Christ as a young woman. When her family learned of her conversion, her mother locked her in her bedroom. Not for a day. Not for a week. For two years!

She was not allowed to talk or eat with her brothers and sisters because of her "infidel" status. Radio provided her only connection to the outside world and to her faith. Although her parents thought she was listening to secular music, she actually tuned in to shortwave Christian programs from Europe. As she listened, she wrote down Bible verses on scraps of paper and then hid them in her clothes or pillow when she wasn't memorizing them.

Eventually, her parents began letting her out for short periods of time; beyond that, they still treated her much like a prisoner. One of Hoda's cousins was a believer, although few people knew it. Learning of Hoda's predicament, he mentioned his cousin's plight to Naasir, a friend in his tightly knit Christian circle.

Naasir was inspired by Hoda's faith and frustrated by her lack of freedom. After contemplating her situation and praying about it, he determined to rescue her. For two years, he saved money in order to liberate her from her bedroom prison. For two years, he prayed about his plan. Finally, it was time to put it into motion.

With Hoda's permission, Naasir asked her parents for their daughter's hand in marriage. Her parents knew little about him, only that he was tall, dark-haired, and handsome. They presumed he was a Muslim although they never asked. Deciding this was the perfect solution for ridding their daughter of her "infidel" status, they consented to the marriage.

Naasir and Hoda fell in love, were married, and vowed to do all they could to share their faith in Christ with others. But the furnace of persecution remained hot.

Muslims often harassed and mocked them. Muslim landlords evicted them. The birth of their son was a joyful blessing, yet one that added pressure to find a stable living situation. After a move to yet another apartment, the couple's worn and wobbly furniture fell apart. They had no food. The weather turned cold. They slept on the floor. All of this they did gladly because "we felt God was preparing us to trust us with a ministry," Naasir said.

Despite the uncertainties of their life in Egypt, they have remained faithful to their calling. Naasir teaches others how to share God's Word. Hoda helps shelter women who have been evicted from their homes after placing their trust in Christ. Ultimately, other Christians helped Naasir and Hoda find a permanent living situation.

In addition to the ever-present threat of being found out by authorities, they still experience friction with their Muslim families. Now that their son attends school, they face a new and difficult challenge. Every day he encounters resistance to the Christian life and faith he experiences at home. He gets confused when he hears something at school that is different from what his parents have taught him. In school, they teach him that Christians are infidels and even to curse Christ. At home, Naasir and Hoda try to correct it.

"We have had many chances to leave Egypt," Hoda said, "but we are convinced that we have to be in Egypt to complete our ministry here."

Despite serious opposition, Naasir and Hoda courageously embody Mark 8:35: "For whoever would save his life will lose it, but whoever loses his life for my sake and the gospel's will save it." They are reminded constantly that the Word of God never promises physical safety—just strength and wisdom from God for whatever comes their way.

We can learn so much from them.

"In Egypt, our theology is the theology of pain," Naasir explained. "We don't know the theology of prosperity, but we know Jesus."

Naasir and Hoda know that hope, contentment, and peace can be found only in Jesus Christ. So instead of trying to construct a life free from physical harm, they courageously trust God for whatever lies ahead as they serve as his witnesses in Egypt. They are committed to do his will, not their own. May we do the same.

10

FROM PERSECUTOR TO PERSECUTED

Abdulmasi
Nigeria

After bombing a church, Abdulmasi liked to return to the scene to relish his work. To learn the body count. To bask in the glory of killing Christians. This was, after all, a major focus of the fanatical group Jama'atu Nasril Islam, in which he participated.

Decades ago, his comrades began calling him "Mr. Insecticide." He earned this nickname because he was, "the only one who could organize the killing of insects—the killing of Christians," he explained. "When you were looking for someone to get rid of insects, then call me. This was my life."

Whenever Muslims in northern Nigeria felt Christians were encroaching, they would call him. He specialized in car bombs, riot planning, and infiltrating Christian organizations, the last of which proved to be his undoing—or, from a biblical perspective, his redemption.

Abdulmasi had known no other life than absolute adherence to Islam. When he was five, his family forced him into *almajiri*, an antiquated Islamic practice popular in West Africa. Muslim families send their young sons to a local imam. A boy doing *almajiri* might join forty or fifty other young boys in the imam's instruction. Their days are as rigid as those of prisoners.

In the morning, the boys recite the Quran in Arabic, a language they do not understand. They recite it for hours, and literally for years, until they memorize the Quran. The task is not unlike an English-speaking child memorizing the Bible in Chinese.

At midday, the boys walk the streets and beg for food, which they share first with the imam. Afterward, they might study the Hadith, a collection of sayings ascribed to the prophet Muhammad and written by Islamic scholars beginning in the ninth century. In radicalized Islamic sectors around the world, the Hadith is the source from which young boys learn the concepts of jihad, paradise, and killing enemies of Allah.

Abdulmasi lived on a steady diet of this for a decade. "Islam is a teaching of hatred—hatred and nothing more than hatred," he declared. "If there is any evil in society, they will relate it as a result of Christians." His only solace in this life? A promise of "paradise" if he killed enemies of Allah.

At age seventeen, wanting desperately to escape a life he hated, Abdulmasi became involved in his first jihad against Christians in the city of Bauchi, Nigeria. The jihadis did not touch women or children, but they did beat and slash men. During this attack, Abdulmasi spotted a known Christian coming out of his home.

"I began beating his legs so he couldn't run away," Abdulmasi recalled. "He fell down and my boys attacked him, trying to kill him. A seven-year-old boy was the one who slaughtered the man with a knife. Pressing down on his neck, he cut the man. They called the boy 'Chief Slaughterer.'"

After the killing, Abdulmasi rejoiced. "You see, when you do this, when you kill a mosquito," he said, clapping his hands together, "you have achieved something. You smile even though you see blood on your hands. I have gotten rid of the enemy of Allah, my enemy too."

Years passed. The killings continued. One day Abdulmasi returned to a church he had just bombed only to find something odd happening. Church members who had survived the attack were singing. This infuriated Abdulmasi. When he returned to the mosque, he lamented what he had seen. "They are rejoicing," he huffed. "They are happier." *Why couldn't I rid these mosquitoes from the church?* he wondered.

In frustration, he decided to use a new tactic. He would infiltrate the church as an impostor and look for ways to kill Christians. The next day, he went to the church and told the pastor, "I'm a Muslim, but I want to become a Christian."

The pastor and his congregation eagerly embraced Abdulmasi. "The love I was shown surprised me."

He began attending services regularly. He joined the young adult group, went to baptism class, and was baptized. All the while, he was secretly returning to the mosque to pray and fast.

For six years, Abdulmasi lived this double life. He might bomb a church across town one day and lead a Bible study the next. He was even appointed the young adult leader. But when the church planned a conference and invited a prominent pastor to talk, Abdulmasi was furious. *Why not me? Am I not the young adult leader? Why wasn't I asked to speak?*

He attended the conference, anger churning inside. He specifically prayed the speaker would fail and that he would be asked to take over. But God had a different plan for Abdulmasi. During the last day of the conference, the pastor spoke on 1 Kings 18, Elijah's challenge to the prophets of Baal.

"How long are you going to waver between two opinions?" the pastor thundered. "If God is God, worship him. If Baal is god, worship him."

Abdulmasi perked up.

"Who are you deceiving?" the pastor pressed. "How long now since that day you said you have accepted Christ and you have not been serious? Why are you playing this double game?"

Abdulmasi squirmed. *This man knows about me! Who told him? Soon he will call out my name.*

"Just humble yourself," the pastor continued. "Just stand up. Let me pray for you, and the Lord will forgive you for all you have been doing. Forget that you are an armed robber. Forget that you are a killer. Forget all those things. Stand up!"

Abdulmasi stood up. His double life ended. When he went forward to profess his faith in Christ—this time for real—he began a new life in God's grace. He also opened himself up to retribution from the jihadis with whom he had previously aligned.

"Don't go near the mosque," one of the boys later warned him. "They will kill you."

Meanwhile, the church elders were delighted to hear of his commitment but stunned at the revelation of his double life. "What do we do with this man?" they debated. "Oust him? Embrace him?" They prayed for three days.

Their decision? They would hide him to save his life. "My son," the pastor told Abdulmasi, "God is going to use you mightily."

And God has used him. While hiding at the home of another pastor, Abdulmasi could not help but share his faith with Muslims. He always looked for opportunities to introduce Muslims to Christ—and always looked over his shoulder.

Months became years. Years became decades. Abdulmasi married. He and his wife had children. But his jihadi past would not be forgotten. He was still a marked man. On one occasion, when Muslims surrounded his house, he narrowly escaped death by slipping out a back way. Three years later, Muslims confronted his college-age son.

"We have not come to rob you," one said. "We have come to kill you because you are your father's son." And they slit his throat.

"It was very difficult," said Abdulmasi, "but there is no sacrifice that is too big for God."

Demonstrating great courage, Abdulmasi reached out to share Christ with the man who had helped plan his son's death. The man rebuffed Abdulmasi; however, the man's son heard about what happened and showed up at Abdulmasi's house.

"Please," he said, "tell me about your Christ."

It is never too late for God to redeem us. Looking back at a life in which he persecuted Christians, lived a double life, and then was persecuted himself, Abdulmasi can only shake his head. "If you want to win Muslims," he said, "you have to love them, not with the human type of love, but the love you, yourself, have experienced through Christ. People are seeing me share my real heart now. If it were not for the grace of God, I would not be who I am."

The change in Abdulmasi from persecutor to persecuted reflects a step of courage that makes a powerful impact. As the apostle Paul wrote in Galatians 1:23–24, "They only were hearing it said, 'He who used to persecute us is now preaching the faith he once tried to destroy.' And they glorified God because of me."

It is never too late for any of us to run into God's arms. Pray for those who persecute our brothers and sisters in Christ, who have known nothing but a life of hatred. Ask that they be introduced to the God of love and forgiveness through Christ's atoning work on the cross. Pray that they, like Abdulmasi, will have the courage to embrace Christ and leave the killing behind. Take time right now to pray.

11

COURAGE TO KEEP WALKING

Sajid
Pakistan

Hours had passed since Sajid, a twenty-seven-year-old evangelist, boarded a bus to go share the gospel in one of Pakistan's more dangerous areas. As the bus rumbled along, he chatted with several passengers seated near him. Despite the fact that Muslim extremists in this area prowled for followers of Christ like lions seeking prey, Sajid began talking about Jesus.

What gave him the courage to speak so openly? When he attended Bible school years earlier, Sajid had dreamed that a large open door stood at the entrance to one of Pakistan's prominent cities. He believed the dream was God's way of guiding him in opening new doors for the gospel. During the decade following that dream, Sajid led hundreds of Pakistanis to Christ.

A bearded man seated nearby shook his head. "You Christians do not consider anything about our prophet, so why should we listen to you talk about your Bible?"

Sajid measured his response and resisted any attempt to be impolite. But as 1 Peter 3:15 says, he was prepared to defend the reason for his faith. "Our Bible," he answered, "makes no reference to your prophet."

"The prophet was written in your Bible!" the man retorted angrily. "But you people would not accept it. You changed the words to your own!"

Realizing it would be futile to continue, Sajid ended the conversation.

Shortly after Sajid got off the bus, about a dozen men grabbed him, blindfolded him, and shoved him into the backseat of a car. Twenty-five minutes later, he was dumped at a compound where other people began questioning him.

"Who are you?" the leader demanded. "Are you a preacher? Are you converting Muslims? Which organization do you belong to?"

Sajid fell silent with fear.

"Are you mute?" another asked. "We will kill you if you don't answer our questions."

"I am telling you the truth," Sajid responded. "I am God's preacher."

"If you want us to spare your life, you must deny your faith and become a Muslim. If you don't do as we say, we will torture you. Within thirty minutes, your passion for Christianity will blow away like dust in the wind."

"I am ready for whatever you choose to do to me," Sajid declared. "I am prepared to die for Jesus. I will not lose my passion for him no matter what you do to me."

Sajid's kidnappers strapped him to a tree, tied his hands behind him, and forced him to stand barefoot on a block of ice. While the Pakistani heat bore down on him, baking the rest of his body, his feet tingled in pain—as if he were standing on a million pins.

Half an hour became an hour. An hour became two hours. Two hours became four. The bottoms and lower sides of Sajid's feet swelled into blisters, tinted in green. He wept but did not speak. Sweat poured from his body, staining his clothes.

"Look," jeered one of the many onlookers. "It is a hundred degrees, and the Jesus lover has frostbite!" The crowd laughed.

"Maybe now you will give up this futile running after Jesus and return to where you belong," a tormentor said. "Maybe now you will return to Allah."

Sajid shook his head.

"Then you will be following Jesus on stumps!" the man replied. "When your feet crumble, we will ice down your nubs. When your nubs freeze, we will saw them off. Jesus will turn and look for you, but you will not be there because you will be a man with no legs! Ha! But if you follow Allah, you will not only walk but also run. Isn't that the better option?"

Again, Sajid shook his head.

"Jesus," he cried out, after hours of ice torture. "Help me. Help me, Jesus!"

Sajid later recalled what happened next. "Suddenly, I saw a vision of a radiant angel appearing in front of me. Jesus was with me, like the fourth man when Shadrach, Meshach, and Abednego were in the fiery furnace."

His pain eased. He gained strength. To the surprise of his tormentors and the crowd mocking him, he began singing worship songs. Then he blacked out.

Sajid awoke in the middle of the night lying in a drainage ditch alongside a dirt road. His wallet and a Hebrew language book he'd been carrying sat beside him. A passerby, a modern-day Good Samaritan, checked him in to a local hotel and paid for him to stay for three days while he recovered. Afterward, Sajid's brother took him for medical treatment and then home to rest.

Sajid's tormentors stated that without feet Sajid would be unable to follow Jesus, yet today he is still walking—and still talking—about his beloved Savior.

Jesus never promised a life of ease on earth to those who serve him. But he did promise that he would not abandon us. When he sent his disciples out into the world to spread the gospel, as Sajid was doing, Jesus promised, "And behold, I am with you always, to the end of the age" (Matthew 28:20).

The very presence of Jesus with us in the midst of our suffering gives us courage to press on when our own strength fails us.

Let's join others—people like Sajid—in God's global family to serve Christ with our eyes set firmly on him.

Father, thank you for Sajid's example of courageous faith. As I face my "block of ice" for the activity of my faith, may I stand strong in the face of opposition, using each circumstance to declare the truth of Christ to those watching. In Christ's name, Amen.

12

STEPPING UP TO
THE PODIUM

Emily
Bangladesh

Emily stood as her principal introduced her to the rest of her school. He needn't have bothered; everyone already knew who she was—and what she was.

And they could hardly wait for her to make her speech.

Too nervous to scan the sea of faces, Emily heard rather than saw her six hundred classmates gathered for the school assembly. Some were already laughing, just like they always did. Or pointing at her, like they always pointed.

Emily laid her carefully prepared speech on a small podium, smoothing the papers flat.

Be with me, God, she prayed silently.

Then Emily looked up and began talking.

There'd been no hope for a smooth transition when twelve-year-old Emily arrived at her new school three years earlier. She was the new kid, but that was just a sliver of the problem.

Most of her fellow students were Muslims, and the rest were Hindus. The people of Bangladesh can believe and worship as they please, but just one half of 1 percent are Christians; followers of Christ often encounter opposition. Housing, employment, friendships—they're all in short supply for those who proclaim Jesus Christ, especially those who leave Islam.

Emily was one of only two Christian students at her school, making her an instant outsider—and a target.

She felt the first slap of discrimination almost immediately. Assuming Emily was a Hindu, a teacher asked the new fourth grader if she was allowed to eat beef.

"Of course," Emily replied cheerfully. "Christians are absolutely allowed to eat beef."

Emily didn't realize the group of girls standing nearby overheard her remark. Emily was a Christian *and* in their school? The girls decided something had to be done.

Then it started.

At first the harassment didn't amount to much. Snide comments. Dirty looks. A stolen water bottle. But then some of Emily's classmates began looking for ways to get her expelled.

Emily was shocked. She felt betrayed. As the bullying escalated, she grew angry with her classmates and also her teachers. They knew Emily was being bullied but chose to look the other way.

Eventually, the bullies were insulting Emily and ridiculing her faith. How could she think Jesus Christ was born of a virgin? Didn't she know the Gospels were nothing but myths and lies? Who could believe such nonsense?

In some ways, attacks on her faith hurt Emily more than the personal jabs. The bullies' stinging words hit home, and she sometimes cried herself to sleep.

In fifth grade, Emily finally made a friend: a Muslim girl who accepted Emily despite her Christian faith. When the two girls were together, the bullies circled but didn't bother Emily. Those days Emily was alone, the bullies pounced.

One day six girls surrounded Emily during lunch. One of them asked for a bite of the chicken sausage Emily had brought from home. Confused, Emily handed the girl her food.

As Emily watched, the girl took a bite, slowly chewed it up, and spit it into her hand. Instantly, the other girls grabbed Emily's arms and legs while forcing her mouth open.

Emily thrashed about in an attempt to escape, but the girl with the chewed sausage shoved it into Emily's mouth.

Emily desperately wanted to fight back—so she did. And she was hurt in the process.

When Anjoli picked her daughter up from school that day, she found Emily in tears. Though her mother pressed for an explanation, Emily was too shaken by the attack to even talk about it for several hours.

Emily felt increasingly isolated at school and her grades suffered as a result. On days when her friend was absent from school, Emily hid in a storage closet.

The assault at school was the first physical attack Emily experienced because of her faith, but it wasn't the first time she'd encountered persecution.

When Emily was just a few months old, a mob of fifty people attacked her parents' discipleship training school. Armed with bamboo sticks and machetes, the crowd shattered windows as they hurled insults and shouted threats at the Christian family.

With no way to contact the police and without knowing many people in the city, Emily's father, Barun, and her mother didn't know what to do. They started to pray. Eventually, the banging and shouting stopped.

Barun never discovered what caused the angry mob to disperse, but he considers their departure an answered prayer—one that may have saved the lives of his family.

As Emily walked through her own painful persecution at school, her parents again prayed for God's intervention. But they also encouraged their daughter to stand up—not just for herself but also for her faith.

When she was in sixth grade, Emily's parents brought a request to the school principal: "Since Muslim and Hindu students don't attend school on their religious holidays, could Emily be excused on Christian holidays?" they asked.

In Bangladesh, as in other predominantly Muslim countries, students are out of school on Fridays, the Muslim day of rest, but attend classes on Sundays. And Christian holidays receive no recognition whatsoever.

After Barun and Anjoli repeatedly asked for Emily to be excused for Easter Sunday, the principal surprised them by adding Easter to the school's holiday calendar. She even invited Emily to speak about Easter during a school assembly.

Barun considered this a major win. *Okay, we have a victory. And maybe God will do even more with this.*

He was right.

When first asked to speak about Easter, Emily's anxiety spiked. If bullies persecuted her for quietly being a Christian, what might happen if she stood in front of the entire school talking about Easter? How much worse would things get? Would her sole Muslim friend decide it was all too much and turn away?

But then Emily considered her speech in a new light. It was actually an opportunity, a way to tell her school about Jesus. *No one knows what Easter is or why we celebrate it,* she thought. *I can tell them.*

Barun helped Emily draft her speech, tailoring it to the school's largely Muslim audience who knew Jesus as a prophet—but nothing more. Barun and Emily wrote about Christ's life, teachings, miracles, and death on the cross.

Because she'd been given permission to speak about the significance of Easter, Emily wrapped up her speech with Jesus' resurrection and added an invitation to embrace faith in Christ.

The assembly was held on a Sunday, in an open area just outside the school building. Emily's six hundred classmates were there, as were many of their parents, and fifty school staff. Loudspeakers stood ready to broadcast Emily's words to the audience—and far beyond into the busy neighborhood surrounding the school.

Residents would hear her, as would patrons of nearby shops. A medical school and hospital were close by, so patients and medical personnel would also hear at least snatches of Emily's testimony.

Emily's parents stood just outside the school's gate, beneath a mango tree, listening intently as their daughter was introduced. They knew she had stage fright, and they knew what seizing this chance to courageously stand for Jesus might cost her.

Emily took a deep breath as her principal handed her the microphone. Hands trembling, she bravely launched into her speech.

When she was finished, Emily placed the microphone on the podium, gathered her notes, and returned to her seat.

She steadied herself, preparing for the backlash she was sure was coming.

But the persecution never arrived.

Instead, several Muslim teachers approached Emily with questions. Some asked for a copy of her speech. Two even requested Bibles, which Barun happily supplied.

The girls who'd bullied Emily abruptly stopped the harassment. One even apologized and asked for a Bible. More than a year later, Emily's math teacher attended a Christmas service with Emily's family, who then presented the teacher with a Bible.

Emily's speech continued echoing in the lives of those who heard it—including Emily herself.

Looking back, she says persecution taught her significant lessons. She now understands God is always with her and does, in fact, use all things for his glory. And she's learned challenges can benefit us in ways we don't necessarily see in the moment.

"I think sometimes persecution is actually a way to grow in your faith," Emily says. "When you're persecuted and suffer, you bear sweeter fruit as a result."

Emily, now seventeen, has attended a predominantly Christian boarding school in India for two years. When she graduates, she plans on entering discipleship training before attending a university. Eventually, she hopes to work in full-time ministry, just like her parents.

"That would be an adventure," she says, smiling. "I like adventure. I also like a lot of people getting to know God. It would be a win-win."

When asked how others could follow her example and boldly share the gospel, Emily's response is simple and direct: pray about it, and then trust God for the words to speak.

"Go for it," she says. "Don't be scared."

Notice Emily's advice for sharing the gospel in challenging situations. She doesn't suggest drumming up courage on our own. Instead, she points to God, who's willing to provide both the courage and words needed.

The apostle Paul even needed assurance not to fear. One night in a vision, the Lord said to him, "Do not be afraid, but go on speaking and do not be silent, for I am with you..." (Acts 18:9–10).

For God is with you...that's why we don't have to be afraid when we are his witnesses.

Pray and then rely on God: that's Emily's advice.

And after that?

Go for it. And don't be scared.

13

A MOST UNLIKELY CHANGE

Samrita
Malaysia

Whack!

Her father's backhand caught Samrita on the cheek and sent her flailing to the ground. Again. Her nose began to bleed.

"You are worthless to me, Samrita," he said in a Malaysian dialect slurred by alcohol. "You are worthless to everyone. Like your twelve brothers and sisters."

It was the mid-1990s, and her family was imploding—splintered by fists, alcohol, and words that cut like knives. Her father drank. Her mother cowered in fear, refusing to intervene. And who could blame her? Samrita tried to keep the peace, tried to hold her family together.

"Papa, you don't know what you're saying," Samrita scolded, following another blow from her father. "You don't mean that."

"Oh, poor Samrita," he mocked, "but I *do*." He laughed, shoved a chair at her that bruised her knee, then staggered away to sleep off his night at the bar.

At age eighteen, Samrita started seeing a young Muslim man named Uda. She viewed him as a way out of her father's house, and they married in 1999. Samrita embraced Islam in order to marry, but things did not go well for her. Uda slipped into using drugs and beating her up just as her father had.

"It is as if I am jinxed," she told her friend Aisha.

"You must be more diligent in your devotion to Islam," Aisha replied.

So Samrita began praying five times a day, dressed modestly, recited the Quran, and even planned a pilgrimage to Mecca. But none of these gave her the inner peace she so desperately sought.

Then one day in 2006, a most unlikely change happened. It began with a visit from her father.

Seeing her father jolted Samrita. She gingerly opened the door, fearful memories of her past searing her soul. It had been a long time since she had seen him.

"What do you want?" she asked in a staccato burst of skepticism.

"Only to say one thing to you."

"And what is that?" she asked.

His eyes glistened. Samrita had never seen this look before. Something had changed.

"I am sorry," he stated.

"Papa?"

"I am not worthy to be your father."

Samrita swallowed hard, then asked, "What has happened to you?"

"I am not the man you knew years ago," he said. "I am a changed man."

Her idealism encouraged her to believe him; her memory encouraged her to doubt. "And how do I know this?"

He held out a small box. "For you."

She opened it. Inside was a necklace with a small wooden cross. "Samrita," he said, "I have left my anger, my ego, and my stupidity at the foot of the cross. I am now a Christian."

Samrita did not know exactly what this meant. But as she began to visit her family every month, she discovered her father had indeed changed. He told all of his children what Christ had done in his life and begged their forgiveness.

Although her father's words intrigued Samrita, his actions convinced her that whoever this Christ was, he had power.

Formerly a bully, her father was now gentle. Once belligerent, he was now kind. At one time selfish, he was now selfless.

She began asking about this Jesus, and at a Christian seminar in 2008, she accepted Jesus Christ as her Lord and Savior. She did not tell Uda, however. She had found the peace she had longed for and didn't want to spoil it.

When Uda found her Bible one day, he lashed out. He cursed her and kicked her out of the house for rejecting Islam. Samrita grabbed their two children, ten-year-old Lili and five-year-old Faiz, and took them with her.

Uda felt betrayed and decided to divorce Samrita; he also reported her to the sharia police in charge of administering Islamic law. They ordered her to appear in court before the religious authorities.

Fellow Christians began to fast and pray, asking for God's favor in Samrita's case. If Uda told the court she had left Islam, Samrita could be sentenced to three years in a walled detention center, euphemistically called a "purification center." There, Muslims would try to convert her back to Islam. If she refused to go to the center, she would face prison.

During the trial, the judge repeatedly asked Uda why he wanted a divorce. Strangely, he refused to answer, even though doing so would have likely meant a prison sentence for Samrita. The judge granted the divorce, awarding the two children to Uda with no visitation rights for Samrita. But she would not go to prison.

Samrita now attends a Malaysian church with sixty members. She and her father are closer than ever. His love of Jesus became *their* love of Jesus. She has forgiven her father and Uda for abusing her.

Although Uda allows Samrita to visit the children, he has warned her not to share her faith with them. Despite the risk of losing all contact with her son and daughter, Samrita has the courage to do it anyway.

"With help from the Lord, I will have the right to take care of my kids," she said. Meanwhile, she lives with the confidence that

nothing is beyond God's power. And this truth gives her courage
to trust her future to Jesus.

*Samrita has seen that Christ indeed makes all things new, as
2 Corinthians 5:17 promises: "Therefore, if anyone is in Christ, he is a
new creation. The old has passed away; behold, the new has come." She
is reminded of this wonderful truth each time she puts on the wooden
cross necklace her father gave her.*

*May we also trust in our new identity in Christ and boldly pro-
claim his gospel, no matter the cost.*

14

A KNOCK AT THE DOOR

Ramtin Soodmand
Iran

Ramtin Soodmand and his wife, Mitra, were enjoying a relaxing evening at home, simply sitting together and watching a movie. As leaders of an underground church movement in Tehran, they were accustomed to full days teaching, preaching, and encouraging fellow believers.

But then came a knock at the door.

When Ramtin carefully cracked open his door, sixteen plain-clothes intelligence officers pushed into the apartment Ramtin and Mitra shared with their two children.

The policemen immediately took the couple's cellphones, and one ordered Mitra to put on a head covering and long coat.

Other officers shut windows and pulled curtains closed so no neighbors could see or hear what came next. Officers then fanned out to rifle through the couple's possessions, tipping books off shelves and emptying cabinets. One officer silently filmed the raid.

The police ransacked the room, confiscating boxes of Bibles, Christian books, laptops, and anything else that might prove useful in their investigation.

Drawn by the noise, twenty-year-old Ramita edged out of her bedroom to see what was happening. Immediately, she was shoved next to her parents as the search continued. Mitra and Ramita both cried as they endured the men's shouting.

It was chaos.

The couple's seventeen-year-old son, Rayan, was shocked by what he found when he returned home. Mitra tried comforting her children as two officers led Ramtin to a bedroom for questioning. Ramtin's family had no way of knowing what would happen behind that closed door.

Ramtin's interrogation lasted for hours. During that time, officers tried to speak to the children alone, but Mitra wouldn't allow it. At one point, Ramita shamed the officers for ruining others' lives.

"We don't enjoy the situation either," one officer admitted.

Eventually, Mitra was led to the bedroom to join Ramtin. The interrogators proposed a compromise that might save the pair.

"We know everything," they told the couple. "If you cooperate with us, you will not go to prison, and we will not restrict your ministry." They knew Ramtin was a key leader in the Iranian church, and they were aware of Mitra's involvement.

But, the officers explained, there was a way out.

The government was prepared to make Ramtin a "legitimate" pastor. They would give him a church building and provide him with a congregation. The church could even meet openly.

There was one catch: the church would have to follow government directives, and the congregation would be handpicked by the government.

Ramtin was to parrot the government's claim that Iran had complete religious freedom, that people of all backgrounds—including Muslims—were free to join the church.

"There are many pastors inside Iran and outside Iran who cooperate with us," they told Ramtin. "You are not the first person. This is a good opportunity for you to improve your lifestyle."

That was the carrot the interrogators dangled in front of the couple, but they also carried a big stick.

"And if you don't cooperate, you will be arrested."

"So you are asking us to spy?" Mitra responded. "If so, we aren't those kinds of people."

"You have two minutes to discuss our offer and make a decision," the police said, turning up the pressure. "Either Ramtin will be arrested immediately, or he will appear two days later at our office to begin his work."

The couple knew Ramtin probably couldn't survive prison or torture; he struggled with diabetes and heart problems. In the end, Ramtin and Mitra both signed a document stating Ramtin would meet with authorities in two days.

Then, five hours after storming into the apartment, the officers left at 2:00 a.m. carrying everything needed for a quick conviction.

But Ramtin had no intention of accepting the government's offer. "I cannot cooperate with the devil army," he said. He had agreed to the meeting only to avoid instant arrest. He now had forty-eight hours to find a way out of his predicament.

And the clock was ticking.

Ramtin knew what was in store if he refused to serve as a puppet pastor. He'd already spent more than nine weeks in prison and forty days in solitary confinement for his Christian work.

And while Ramtin wasn't afraid of prison, he was concerned for his family. Rayan hadn't yet completed his junior year of high school, and Ramita was a college student. They needed him in their lives, but they also needed to see his courage in choosing Christ, no matter what.

Ramtin had no illusions about how cruel the Iranian regime could be to Christians. When he was sixteen, his father, Rev. Hossein Soodmand, was executed by the government for apostasy. Ramtin's mother, who was blind, was left alone to care for him and his three siblings.

All Christian activity in the Islamic Republic of Iran has been illegal since 1979, and the law forbids any Muslim from leaving Islam. Christian converts are jailed on charges such as "propaganda against the regime" and "acting against national security."

Even owning a Bible and talking about Christ are punishable offenses.

Yet, in spite of ruthless persecution, biblical churches in Iran continue to grow. In fact, they remain one of the fastest growing in the world—a source of concern for government officials. The very officials who had discovered Ramtin's ongoing Christian work.

In two days' time, the Iranian government expected Ramtin to assume his role as a sham pastor. But with God's help, he would never take the job...and the house churches would continue.

Should any Christian be arrested and potentially expose the whole network, Ramtin and other house church leaders had developed careful methods of working one on one. Knowing he could be arrested or killed, Ramtin had told the director of an Iranian theological seminary that he wanted to coach others to take over his work. "I do not know how long I have to live or what persecutions might come across my path," he had told the director two years earlier. "But if this happens or if they put me in prison, I would like to prepare several people for the work of the Lord. I would like to pass on to them a knowledge of all my methods and experiences of ministry so they can take my place and continue with the work of the Lord in order that the work of the house churches will not cease."

But now, Ramtin turned his attention to the immediate problem: getting himself and his family out of danger.

Ramtin and Mitra assumed the intelligence officers had planted listening devices in their home, so they didn't openly discuss what they'd do next. Instead, they scratched notes to one another as they considered options.

Ramtin loved Iran deeply, as did his children. He knew they'd suffer if the family left, but his children faithfully wrote, "Dad, do according to how God leads you."

Together the family decided Ramtin would flee the country immediately, and in time they would follow. Ramtin quietly made arrangements to be smuggled over the border.

Then he and Mitra wandered side by side through Tehran, talking quietly. They knew they were being followed, and even a quick embrace might tip off officials Ramtin was fleeing. Finally, the couple said their goodbyes and went their separate ways, clinging to the hope God would reunite them.

A few months later, that hope was fulfilled. Ramtin and his family now live in a different country. They're safe, but doubts about leaving Iran sometimes tug at Ramtin.

For thirty years he served courageously, risking everything to follow Christ in one of the world's most dangerous countries. Now Ramtin's living with a different sort of courage: courage to trust that God is working all things for the good of those who love him.

It takes courage to trust God when it's hard to understand his plan for your life. When illnesses don't get better. When people you love suffer. When plans unravel, and danger knocks at your door.

Ramtin's courage was borne out of trusting in God's faithfulness and love. He continues to trust God's faithfulness and love.

Four young Hebrews refused to betray God by bowing in worship to King Nebuchadnezzar. By making this choice, they trusted God even as they were thrown into a fiery furnace, the consequence of their disobedience to the king (Daniel 3).

How does trusting God's faithfulness and love inspire you to courage when it is hard to understand God's plan for your life?

15

JUST GIVING OUT BIBLES

Boutros
Syria

Boutros had not returned home for the 4:00 p.m. curfew imposed in his village. It was unsafe for anyone to be on the streets—especially a man who handed out Bibles and talked with Syrians about Jesus. He was easy prey for Muslim extremists who decried anything or anyone opposing Islam or Muhammad.

"Boutros," a church leader said to him days earlier, "you must stop this, at least for now. We cannot afford to lose you. It is too dangerous."

"But this is what I'm called to do," he replied. "To spread the good news of Christ to the thirsty Syrians."

"Yes, but there is kidnapping and torturing," the church leader countered. "The extremists are cutting Christians into pieces."

Boutros had refused to stop sharing Jesus.

By late evening, church leaders and other Christians began thinking the worst. People gathered to pray for their friend. Calls to Boutros' cell phone triggered no response. They had no way of knowing his phone had been turned off.

"The image that came to mind," said one friend, "was that Boutros, like the others, had been cut to pieces."

At 9:00 p.m., Boutros' fellow believers were so desperate for news they even called the city's secret police to see if they had arrested him.

"Why was he out on the streets?" they asked.

"Giving out Bibles," they replied.

"Why was he doing that?" the policeman asked. "Is he crazy?"

After the secret police claimed to know nothing about Boutros' whereabouts, his friends became even more concerned. "It was a dark moment for us," recalled a friend who was among those praying. "Lord," someone cried out, "he is in your hands. Keep him safe. Protect him."

Morning came. No Boutros.

A full day passed. No Boutros.

Two days passed. No Boutros.

Finally, the entire congregation gathered in the church, so spent they did not even have the energy to eat.

A sudden noise at the door froze them in fear. It swung open. In walked Boutros. The congregation enveloped him in tearstained hugs.

Tired, unshaven, and dirty, he told them about being picked up by the secret police.

"Get out of here," an officer had said, "or we will take you away and you will be gone."

So, Boutros left that street but not the area. He simply walked one street over and began visiting shop after shop to share about Jesus Christ. He knew being salt and light for Jesus required action—not quitting when people opposed his plans.

The police followed him, placed a black bag over his head, and whisked him away to a prison cell crowded with long-bearded Muslim extremists who had run afoul of the secret police.

"Why are you here?" one asked.

"For sharing the love of Christ," Boutros replied, "which I'd like to share with you too."

And that is exactly what he did.

The next day, the head of the secret police sat across from Boutros and angrily interrogated him.

Boutros responded with love, not like-minded anger. "I was just giving out Bibles," he said. "The Bible teaches us to pray for our leaders and respect them."

At these words, the officer calmed down. Boutros looked him in the eye and said, "God is love. And he loves you."

These words ended the interrogation. The officer scribbled down a phone number and slid it to Boutros.

"What is this?"

"My personal cell phone number. Let me know if you have any more trouble with the secret police."

Boutros thanked the man who had released him, then stopped by the church to shower. After sharing his story, he headed home to his wife and child. The next day, he was back on the streets, proclaiming the gospel to all who would listen.

Christians like Boutros risk everything to spread God's Word, even putting their lives in danger. Their stories of courage inspire us as we remember that Jesus said, "I have said these things to you, that in me you may have peace. In the world you will have tribulation. But take heart; I have overcome the world" (John 16:33).

Think of people you know who resist the gospel, as the secret police officer presumably did before he encountered Boutros. Pray that God will speak to their hearts so they will come to know and serve him. After all, God sees in them (as he does in each believer) the potential to exhibit what he sees in Boutros: a courageous faith that will not be deterred.

16

THE COST
OF CHANGE

Mustafa
Morocco

When Mustafa heard his younger brother, Omar, left Islam to become a Christian, anger swiftly launched him into action.

Mustafa snatched up Omar's Bible and other Christian literature. He then rushed outside and burned it all, watching pages of the Bible—a book he considered unclean—curl with flame and fall to ash.

Mustafa loved Omar, but his hatred for Christians forbade him from sharing a house with an apostate. So, Mustafa threw Omar out.

Hoping to bring his wayward brother back to Islam, Mustafa stayed in contact with Omar and eventually asked him for a Bible, thinking he could point out its many errors. Maybe that would show Omar just how foolish he was to turn his back on the truth.

Omar gladly handed Mustafa a Bible—and a pen. He suggested Mustafa mark any verses he found problematic, and they would talk about them.

Mustafa accepted the Bible...and the challenge.

But the more he read, the more Mustafa felt torn between Islam and Christianity. So, when at last he encountered Matthew 7:7, "Ask, and it will be given to you; seek, and you will find; knock, and it will be opened to you," he took a radical step.

He set the Bible down so he could talk to God.

"God, where are you?" he asked. "If you are the one who governs all the world around us, you can tell me the truth. Which is true—the Bible or the Quran?"

A few nights later, Mustafa had a vision in which he tumbled into a deep hole in the ground. Unable to escape, he squinted up from the darkness at a man whose face was obscured by light. The man reached down, pulled Mustafa to safety, and embraced him.

When the vision faded, Mustafa felt at peace. Once again, he opened the Bible and read Matthew 7:7. Except this time he understood what the passage was telling him. *The person who held my hand and gave me a hug was Jesus!*

Two months later, Mustafa left Islam and placed his faith in Christ. His Muslim wife, Salma, later became a Christian too. But as Mustafa and his wife grew close together in Jesus Christ, Mustafa's mother and siblings grew bitter toward him. By leaving their family's religion, they felt *he* had abandoned *them*.

Their decisions to follow Christ came just as the Moroccan government was tightening restrictions. Christian foreigners, including those who had hired Mustafa to work at their Christian-run orphanage, were suddenly expelled from the country.

That cost Mustafa his job—and meant he, too, came under scrutiny.

One day Mustafa received a call ordering him to report to the police station. As soon as Mustafa arrived, an officer asked, "What religion are you following?"

"Christianity," Mustafa answered.

"My reports show there are no Christians living in your community," the policeman responded. Somehow, Salma and Mustafa's brother had managed to evade detection.

"I am willing to be arrested for being a Christian," Mustafa declared.

The officer let him go.

But a week later, Mustafa received orders to return to the station; this time he was told to bring his wife.

Mustafa, Salma, and Omar were now officially a problem.

The interrogations lasted all day. At times, Mustafa and Salma were questioned separately, other times together. As the day dragged on, Mustafa saw God keep his promise to put the right words in their mouths so they could answer boldly, bravely, and with integrity.

The couple experienced what Christ promised in Luke 12:12, "for the Holy Spirit will teach you in that very house what you ought to say." Mustafa knew his wife did not have a lot of biblical knowledge, but she was answering the investigators' questions with wisdom.

At the end of the day, the exhausted husband and wife were sent home.

Two weeks passed before the next interrogation. This time it was conducted by Moroccan intelligence officers who tried luring Mustafa and Salma back to Islam with financial incentives.

When that didn't work, Mustafa's interrogators alternated between beating him and acting like long-lost friends—all attempts to pry information about work he and fellow Christians were doing in Morocco. All the while, Mustafa and Salma clung to God's Word.

Again, the two were released, but this time with an under-standing hanging in the air: at any moment, they could again be pulled in for questioning…beatings…or worse.

Interrogations continued for years. But, in the end, officials asked only that Mustafa describe his Christian faith in writing.

It was essentially a confession.

Police spread the word Mustafa and Salma had turned their backs on Islam. Friends became foes, and relatives and acquain-tances turned into adversaries. Islamists followed the couple, looking for any sign of Christian activity to report.

Yet, in the midst of pressure and persecution, Mustafa and Salma received a delightful gift. They had long prayed for a child, and at last God surprised them with a son.

Mustafa's former supervisor from the orphanage was allowed to visit Morocco and dropped in to see Mustafa. As the old friends shared tea, Mustafa glanced out the window and saw an angry crowd gathering. Local Muslims had seen the foreigner enter

Mustafa's home and were protesting. Some had even reported to the police that an evangelist was visiting Moroccan Christians.

Though Mustafa and Salma felt increasingly alone in their faith, God's presence comforted and sustained them. They would pray together, providing spiritual bread for one another that would give hope and life.

Mustafa and his family eventually relocated near a larger city where he enrolled in seminary. He and Salma established a church for new Christian converts from Islam. Mustafa loves meeting new Christians and teaching those who face persecution—many of whom once hated Christianity as much as he did.

Despite the joys of ministering to new believers, Mustafa and Salma have struggled to raise their son amid the dominant Muslim culture in Morocco. Their son made a commitment to Christ, but his Muslim teachers have tried to influence his thinking.

Still, the couple are committed to the Great Commission and urge Christians around the world to share in that commitment. "The message of the Lord is clear: 'Go make disciples.'" Mustafa and Salma continue to courageously share the gospel—which Mustafa once tried so hard to disprove—with any who will listen.

Some of Jesus' parting words to his disciples were: "Go therefore and make disciples of all nations, baptizing them in the name of the Father and of the Son and of the Holy Spirit, teaching them to observe all that I have commanded you. And behold, I am with you always, to the end of the age" (Matthew 28:19–20).

Mustafa courageously followed where God led, taking the gospel with him. That journey included police interrogations and rejection from his family. But all along the way, Mustafa knew God was with him, just as he is today. "If you hold the Scripture and read it as the loving word of God, it will be with you in any time," Mustafa said.

Mustafa is inviting us to join him in that journey of sharing the gospel.

Pray for courage—and thank God for Mustafa's example.

17

LIVING THE NORMAL CHRISTIAN LIFE

Christian Youth
India

The girls were happy and excited as they returned to their village following several days of discipleship training. Their enthusiasm was dampened, however, when they learned their absence had created quite the stir in their predominantly Muslim village.

Rumors were circulating. One in particular caught the attention of Islamists: the girls had been whisked away to a nearby city to be used for deviant sexual purposes. If that were the case, consequences would be harsh. The young ladies were immediately rounded up and interrogated.

Fearing the girls might be taken from their families and forced into marriages with Islamic extremists as sex slaves because of the initial rumors, a Christian man named Ali handed one of the Islamists a micro-SD card.

"This is what it's all about," Ali told them. "This is why they left."

When one of the Islamists reviewed the content on the SD card, he expected to find pornography. Instead, he heard the gospel. "This isn't so bad," he told the other Islamists who had gathered to question the girls. "It's about Isa (Jesus)."

In that moment, Ali felt the Spirit's nudge to boldly proclaim Christ.

"Repent! Come out of the darkness," Ali pleaded to the radicals and village elders who had gathered.

Realization suddenly dawned on the Muslims: the teaching was about Jesus of the Bible, not the Quran's prophet Isa. Tempers flared.

And Ali's desperate attempt to save his daughters would come at a high price. He would either lose them to a false accusation, or he could defend their honor by boldly proclaiming his family's faith in Christ.

As a small minority in the area, Christians must keep their faith secret. Believers often hide their Bibles, understanding that their discovery by Muslim neighbors could result in violence. Persecution in this community has involved burning down houses, beatings, removing people from their homes, and Christians being kicked out of their families.

The Islamists decided on the spot to reconvert the girls to Islam.

No matter what it took.

The young Christians were rushed to a boarding school on the Islamists' compound, without a chance to gather personal hygiene products or additional clothing. Soon after they arrived, they were herded to a cold, windowless room—their shared quarters until they would be separated from the comfort of one another's presence.

Students and staff at the school snidely called the girls "Christians," not because of the girls' faith but because they were considered infidels. But the young ladies were ready—they had learned during discipleship training that persecution would likely happen as they followed Christ.

One day the girls were escorted to a room where they were interviewed separately by schoolteachers heavily influenced by radical Islam.

Aiming to catch the girls in a lie, the teachers were the ones who were caught off guard by the girls' consistency in their responses and their courage.

During one interrogation, a teacher asked one of the young ladies if she had a cross tattooed on her body. Muslims in the area assume all Christians carry such a mark, and the teacher wanted to check for herself.

In a conservative Muslim culture, children are trained not to question authority. But the girl locked eyes with the teacher and responded with a challenge.

"We will take off our clothes and let you look for cross tattoos," she said, "but if we don't have one, you have to agree to take off your clothes and show us you don't have a cross."

Likely shocked at the girl's bold response, the teacher decided not to look for the tattoo.

Another girl suffered with a severe lung condition, and her parents feared she would die without medication. A villager took her medical papers to the boarding school and insisted all the girls be released. "Otherwise," the villager warned, "you will have a dead girl on your hands that will draw negative attention to the school."

Forty-two days after being torn from their families, the young women were finally sent home.

These Christian girls have been shunned, and they have been barred from attending their former schools. They live as outcasts, yet still participate in discipleship training—both in person and weekly over the phone.

But their six weeks of being detained and interrogated did not diminish the girls' faith in Jesus Christ. Instead, it grew. They praised God for providing for them and sustaining them through-out their abduction. The lack of basic necessities, together with their grief over being taken from their families, only served to deepen the girls' relationship with Christ.

Older believers marvel at the young ladies' courage and con-fidence, as well as their obedience to Christ even in the face of ongoing rejection.

Because they, like the girls, know the truth: in some parts of the world, persecution does not stop for Christ-followers. It may ebb and flow, become more or less violent. But until Jesus returns, persecution will remain.

These girls aren't living through a difficult time.

They are living a normal Christian life for obedient witnesses.

First Peter 4:12–14 says, "Beloved, do not be surprised at the fiery trial when it comes upon you to test you, as though something strange were happening to you. But rejoice insofar as you share Christ's sufferings, that you may also rejoice and be glad when his glory is revealed. If you are insulted for the name of Christ, you are blessed, because the Spirit of glory and of God rests upon you."

These young believers were ready: they knew persecution for their witness was not unusual; it was normal, even expected. And the courage they displayed as they were being persecuted wasn't a moment of bravery that they willed themselves to do. It came as a fruit of their complete trust in the One whose glory rests on them.

That's the reality of life for millions of persecuted Christians, your brothers and sisters living in places where it is difficult and dangerous to follow Christ.

Pray for them. And pray for courage as Christ leads you to live and speak for him.

QUESTIONS FOR REFLECTION AND DISCUSSION

COURAGE

1. What is it about courageous actions that captures your attention? Is it the determination of someone that piques your interest? Does the seeming disregard for personal safety surprise you? Is it simply the courageous actions themselves? Or is it the foundation of conviction that drives someone to display bravery in the face of adversity that inspires you?

    a. Compare and contrast human bravery with God-inspired courage. Is there a difference? What is the difference?

    b. Think of a time when you lived courageously. What drove you to act courageously?

2. Emily was in the extreme minority at her school—one of only two Christians among over six hundred students.

    a. What inspires you about Emily's courage to share the Easter story and continually share her faith despite opposition? How (specifically) does Emily's example of bold witness inspire you to be bolder in your own witness this week?

b. The word "encourage" means to "inspire with courage." How did Emily's Christian parents "inspire her with courage" as she prepared to witness boldly for Christ? What might have happened if she didn't have their encouragement? Who inspires your faith toward courageous living? How do they inspire you to be bold in your witness? Whose courage do you inspire? How can you better inspire others with courage?

3. God's Word has much to say about courage and strength in the face of fear and opposition. Read the passages below and note what action follows courage, who or what inspires courage, and any obstacles to courage. (Note: not every passage directly gives answers to all three questions)

a. Joshua 1:6–9

b. Psalm 23:4

c. Mark 6:49–50

d. 2 Timothy 1:7

e. What practical applications can you implement in your life as a result of what you discovered in these verses?

4. Read 1 Peter 5:8–10.

a. Who did Peter say is the real adversary of biblical disciples? What is the goal of this adversary?

b. Reread the first part of verse 10. What is the result of the devil's evil intent? Knowing that suffering (in this world) is a real threat, how does that cause you to think about the spiritual battles you face?

c. Who rescues biblical disciples from their suffering? List and think through or discuss what each of these might look like in the life of a biblical disciple:

    i. Restore

    ii. Confirm

    iii. Strengthen

    iv. Establish

d. When you read "the same kinds of suffering are being experienced by your brotherhood throughout the world" (1 Peter 5:9), how does that truth embolden you to live more courageously for Christ in the face of opposition and suffering?

e. How do the stories you read in this section reflect that God is "the God of all grace" (1 Peter 5:10)? What is God asking you to do in light of his gift of enduring grace?

Pray

Ask God for greater courage as you live for him. Pray for persecuted Christians like those you have read about in this section, that their courage might give testimony to the truth of the gospel.

Part III

JOY

Blessed are you when people hate you and when they exclude you and revile you and spurn your name as evil, on account of the Son of Man! Rejoice in that day, and leap for joy, for behold, your reward is great in heaven; for so their fathers did to the prophets.

LUKE 6:22–23

Joy is probably not the first emotion we associate with persecuted followers of Christ. Many are tortured, abused, and imprisoned without trial. They may have friends and family members who have been killed for their faith. Others are forced to flee their homes, leaving behind everything they own and the communities they love. Some live in crowded refugee camps with no hope of a better life. Yet joy is often what people notice most when they encounter these believers.

How is this possible? How can people who suffer so much be filled to overflowing with joy?

If we take seriously Jesus' teaching and example, as well as the shared experiences of early Christian believers, the presence of joy in the face of persecution might not be so surprising. Jesus taught his followers to rejoice and leap for joy when they are hated, excluded, reviled, and considered evil for his sake. Why? Because they will be blessed and greatly rewarded for their suffering (Luke 6:22–23).

Jesus, no stranger to persecution and unspeakable suffering, modeled such joy in his life: "...who for the joy that was set before him endured the cross, despising the shame, and is seated at the right hand of the throne of God" (Hebrews 12:2). His example is a powerful antidote to discouragement and weariness of heart.

Our human nature tries to avoid suffering at all costs, but James 1:2–3 reminds Christians that suffering has a purpose: "Count it all joy, my brothers, when you meet trials of various kinds, for you know that the testing of your faith produces steadfastness."

Certainly no follower of Christ likes to suffer. But enduring persecution for the sake of Jesus Christ is far bigger than pain and suffering. It is about participating in God's ongoing redemptive work on earth, and the glorious eternity we will spend with him.

Whether we as believers experience joy in the midst of persecution has far more to do with our focus than on the situations we encounter. If our joy depends on happy life circumstances, we are in serious trouble when we are opposed for our bold witness. But the Bible is clear about focusing on a greater reality: "If then you have been raised with Christ, seek the things that are above, where Christ is, seated at the right hand of God. Set your minds on things that are above, not on things that are on earth" (Colossians 3:1–2).

Internalizing the reality that our joy is not dependent upon circumstances makes all the difference for biblical disciples. It changes our perspective completely. It sows seeds of joy that can't help but bloom. And Hebrews 10:32, 34 reminds us of our eternal reward: "You endured a hard struggle with sufferings...and you joyfully accepted the plundering of your property, since you knew that you yourselves had a better possession and an abiding one [in heaven]."

Such deep joy from God sets apart Christians who willingly face persecution for their witness. And that joy has an impact, sometimes leading the persecutors to discover its source in those they oppress. So read on about your brothers and sisters in Christ who count it a privilege to serve him joyfully...and be inspired to do the same.

18

FREEDOM BEHIND BARS

Jon
Malaysia

A light breeze rustled through the palm trees, easing the ever-present heat that is as much a part of life in Malaysia as cold is in the Arctic. In a small suburb of Kuala Lumpur, a city of 1.6 million people and the sixth most visited city in the world, Jon concluded a Bible study with ten other ethnic Malay Christians.

As they said their goodbyes, Jon felt good. The gathering had gone well. March clouds that often dumped buckets of rain were still far in the distance. He looked forward to getting home, where he could turn on his fan and immerse himself in the Word of God.

Even when he saw the SUV speeding toward him, Jon didn't fret. He knew the drill. Since he had converted to Christianity six years earlier, he'd become accustomed to police harassment. Every three months, they made him report to the station. They would urge him to recite Islamic prayers and reembrace the Islamic faith and his ethnic heritage. And every three months, he'd politely refuse.

Three major ethnicities can be found in Malaysia—Malay, Chinese, and native tribes. In addition, the Malaysian government strives to maintain a distinct, indigenous Malay culture that requires all ethnic Malay people to be Muslim. Two sets of laws exist for governing the people. Civil laws govern all citizens. Islamic laws concerning matters of religion, family, property, and inheritance apply only to Muslims.

It's illegal for Malay people to convert to Christianity, and evangelization of Muslims is punishable by fine, imprisonment, or both. When Jon was arrested in 2011, there were no more than one thousand Malay Christians among Malaysia's population of twenty-eight million.

Jon's boldness in following Jesus Christ made him a traitor in the eyes of most Malays. Yet, police interactions with him always followed the same pattern. He even knew exactly where the police chief would hang his hat each day.

When the SUV screeched to a halt, Jon noticed a bit more bravado than usual. Still, he figured it was a routine three-month visit. Seconds later, three men grabbed him, blindfolded him, and threw him into the car. Then they pursued the other Bible study members.

"No, no, no! Don't take them," Jon called out amid the bedlam. "Just take me. Do what you will with me, but leave them out of it."

The leader grabbed Jon's face, thumb on one side and fingers on the other, squeezing it in a vise-like grip. "Our patience with you, rotten *kafir*,[1] has run out. It is time for you to be rehabilitated. To return to what you never should have left—your faith in Allah!"

Islam is more than a religion for indigenous Malays; it is their national identity. Muslims who try to leave Islam can be subjected to many hardships, including imprisonment in rehabilitation camps. So when the policeman used the word *rehabilitated*, Jon could guess what was in store.

Four hours later, he stumbled out of the SUV and into a walled compound in the northern Malaysia jungle near the Thailand border. Razor wire atop the fifteen-foot-high walls ensured no one would be leaving on their own.

Jon had heard of such places. They were called Islamic purification centers and were presented as "voluntary retreat centers" for Muslims who struggled with their faith. But Jon wasn't a voluntary guest. He was bound hand and foot and placed in a small room with three other men; he later learned they also were Christian converts. Then Jon's "purification" began.

Several times a day, long-bearded Islamic scholars interrogated him. They wanted him to chant with them. He refused.

"All I could hear," he said, "was people praying for me." His abusers poured Islamic "holy water" over his head to "cleanse"

---

1. *Kafir* is an Arabic term of derision used by Muslims when referring to non-Muslims. It comes from a root word meaning to cover something. Therefore, to Muslims, a *kafir* is one who sees the truth of Islam but covers it and is considered an enemy of Islam.

him. When that didn't work, they used seven buckets of water. Jon refused to deny Jesus.

"You must embrace Islam again," a scholar declared.

"I will not," Jon replied. "Even if you chop off my head right now, it's okay. I have my God."

Angered by Jon's defiance, "rehab" workers beat him. While he was on the ground, they kicked him in his stomach and back.

"But I didn't feel any pain or humiliation," he recalled. "I believe the Lord came, and I could hear angels and the prayers of my Christian friends. When those men stepped on me and kicked me, that's when I felt the prayers; that's when I felt the presence of God."

After additional beating and kicking failed, the leaders switched to a new method to "cure" Jon. They forced him to sit naked on ice while men shouted verses from the Quran at him. "We are going to kill you if you don't confess the Muslim prayer," one said.

Jon did not reply.

They beat him with a thick bamboo cane. "Say it!" another commanded.

Jon still did not reply.

He was immersed in a vision of Jesus himself being beaten. "I saw the blood of Jesus dripping, and then I heard the gentle voice of the Holy Spirit telling me not to deny Jesus no matter what."

Jon was so full of the Spirit that, at one point during the beatings, he actually began laughing—not to mock his torturers, but to express his joy for the honor of suffering for his Savior. "I was okay with being beaten," he recalled. "They beat Jesus too."

After three days of torture, the religious police released Jon into the custody of local authorities. Members of his church paid his bond, and he once again was rejoicing in his freedom in Christ.

Jon's joy in the midst of his suffering might seem incredible to us. But such a response won't surprise us if we understand the power of faith and trust in Christ. "Do not fear what you are about to suffer," we read in Revelation 2:10. "Behold, the devil is about to throw some of you into prison, that you may be tested, and for ten days you will have tribulation. Be faithful unto death, and I will give you the crown of life."

By faith, Jon availed himself of the fullness of God's power, and his joy in the midst of suffering could not be contained. He didn't prevail because of deft argumentative skills. Or because he was physically stronger than most people. Or because he was craftier. He prevailed because his trust in God never wavered and he never ceased praying—and because other believers prayed for him.

Father, thank you for my brother, Jon, and his testimony of joy in the midst of suffering. I ask for that same perspective for each member of my persecuted Christian family today—that their joy will be complete in Christ and evident to those who oppose them. Grant them strength today. Amen.

19

TESTED BY FIRE

Solomon
Nigeria

Solomon and his father, Inoma, were not attacked by militant Boko Haram insurgents who would sweep down from the north; nor were they assaulted by violent Fulani Islamic militants who hated Christians. No, their assailants were neighbors.

Muslim men, whom the father and son knew and saw each day, suddenly began shooting at them. Like fish in a barrel, Solomon and Inoma darted left and right seeking some sliver of cover. Bullets ricocheted around them. Men wielding machetes joined in the attack. The father and son didn't stand a chance.

A machete slammed down between Inoma's head and shoulder. The left side of his torso collapsed. He died instantly.

Seconds later, Solomon, reeling and in shock, stopped and stared at his father's killer.

"We will not cut you if you turn back to Islam," stated the young man, bloody machete in hand.

"I will not," Solomon replied.

"You are Christian. Where are you going? This is the end of the road. You have only one choice left: follow Islam."

"No," repeated Solomon.

Immediately, he felt liquid splash across his back. Gasoline fumes almost choked him.

"Now will you leave this Jesus for Allah?" the killer asked.

"I will not."

A blow to the back of his head knocked Solomon to the ground. Another attacker revved up a motorcycle and rode it onto Solomon's back, got off, and laid it—engine still running—on top of him. The attackers then ignited his gasoline-soaked shirt. Pinned to the ground by the weight of the motorcycle, Solomon could not escape the flames. Sometime later, his mind foggy and body racked by pain, Solomon vaguely remembered being placed inside a four-wheel-drive vehicle for the agonizing, bumpy ride to the hospital.

Solomon lived, but his back—even after numerous skin grafts—bears the scars of the attack. Doctors have said his pain will never completely subside.

Even after all he has suffered, Solomon does not lament his disfigurement, the difficulty it creates in his job as a carpenter, or that his fiancée fled after the attack. Nor is he bitter or discouraged. "I won't turn back," he said with confidence. "The salvation that I have in Christ was not free but paid with a price. Christ himself suffered to save me, so I feel I am prepared to suffer in persecution for the salvation I have in Christ."

If Solomon were to see his attackers again, which is a real possibility, he would echo Jesus' words from the cross: "Father, forgive them." He wants his attackers to know the God they despise died for their sins too.

Through persecution and suffering, Solomon has gained a faith that is more precious than gold. "Based on what happened to me," he said, "it is a miracle that I survived. I know that my life is in God's hands, so what happened to me has strengthened my relationship with him."

This is the kind of faith in the face of persecution that Peter, Jesus' disciple, described in 1 Peter 1:6–7: "In this you rejoice, though now for a little while, if necessary, you have been grieved by various trials, so that the tested genuineness of your faith—more precious than gold that perishes though it is tested by fire—may be found to result in praise and glory and honor at the revelation of Jesus Christ."

Rejoice in such testing? Yes!

Jesus considered it joy to remain faithful to the cross and die for the sins of all humanity. Around the world, the fires of hatred lick at our persecuted brothers and sisters like Solomon. Yet they stand firm in their faith—no matter the price—and experience a deep trust and joy only known by those who remain faithful to God.

20

DARING TO SPEAK THE TRUTH

Musa
North Africa

The question hung in the air as Musa's heart clenched.

It was a cold February day at the construction site. A coworker and beloved friend had become suspicious of Musa's unwillingness to kneel in prayer at the prescribed hours like everyone else.

"Why don't you take a break when it's time for prayer like the rest of us? It's your right, and you can have some rest."

To many, this question might seem insignificant. But this was North Africa, where Islam rules with a heavy hand. Not participating in religious practices can trigger scorn. Defying the faith can trigger terrible suffering.

This is it, Musa realized. This was the moment he had to decide if he was going to take a stand for Christ. Be a phony or the real deal. All in or all out. After a long pause, he looked his friend in the eye. "Prayer," he began, "is an intimate conversation with God, and it should be done all the time, in my heart, rather than at specific times using the same phrases and postures."

His friend's eyes narrowed. "You can't be serious, can you?" he questioned, then laughed uneasily. "You are joking with me, aren't you, my friend?"

Musa shook his head. He didn't want to hurt his friend, but he would not lie. "I am quite serious. I am a follower of Christ."

His friend glanced around to make sure no one else could hear. Denial turned to surprise, then to anger. "You have lost your mind, Musa!" he exclaimed. "You have become a kafir!"

"I am who God wants me to be," Musa answered confidently. "He wants the same for you. He created you and longs to have a personal relationship with—"

"Shut up, Musa! I am proud to be a Muslim. You don't deserve my friendship."

"But I hope to keep our friendship," Musa replied.

"You are dead to me. I hope you repent and come back to the true way of Allah and his prophet, Muhammad." Then he turned and left.

A few days later, the construction site supervisor called Musa into the office and asked, "Is this true? Are you now a Christian?"

"I am," Musa responded, realizing his friend had betrayed him.

"Then you are fired for proselytizing—"

"But I have not tried to convert anyone."

"Get out," the supervisor ordered. "No pension. No severance. No final month's wages. Begone, you traitor."

As he headed home, Musa reflected on how much easier—
though not better—his life would be had he not chosen to follow
Christ.

Musa began questioning the Muslim religion he'd been raised
with while he was in his early twenties. He had become uneasy
with Islam's view of justice that permitted people to be hurt and
even murdered in the name of Allah. Nearly a decade passed, however, before his doubt led him to faith in Christ.

At the age of thirty-five, married with three children, Musa
did something nobody in his family had ever done: placed his trust
in Christ as his Lord and Savior. From that moment on, he knew
he had become a wanted man. Even if he never doubted his decision to become a Christ-follower, he would always be looking over
his shoulder.

He even feared telling his wife, Farrah, about his faith because
she might leave and take their children. So he prayed that she,
too, would see the wonder of Jesus and embrace him. Musa began
bringing home Christian literature from a library almost one hundred miles away and watching Christian television broadcasts.

When he finally told Farrah about his faith in Jesus, she
recoiled in fear. "What if our relatives find out?" she exclaimed.
"What then?" Soon, however, after seeing a change for the better
in her husband, she invited Jesus into her life. For two years, the
couple told no one about their new faith.

Then Musa was fired from his construction job, and now he
worried about how he would provide for his family. Not long after
he returned home, the phone rang. A man offered Musa another

construction job, which seemed like a miracle. "Could you meet with me this afternoon?"

"I thought it was the answer to my prayers," Musa would later admit. He became uneasy, however, when he realized the meeting location was an abandoned building, not a construction site.

He had come to an ambush, not a job offer. Two men tried to force him to the back of the property, but Musa refused to leave the main road. The men interrogated him about turning his back on Allah. Then they replaced their words with fists—to the stomach, face, and ribs. Musa began to wonder if he would leave the place alive.

Suddenly, a car approached and screeched to a halt. The attackers stopped their beating. A man in the car opened a door and yelled, "Get in! We will help you."

Amazingly, news of Musa's faith and firing already had spread throughout the small Christian community that rallied to help him.

"He is a kafir!" yelled his tormentors as the car sped away. "He is a Christian and an evangelist!"

Days later, the same two assailants showed up in Musa's neighborhood and spread the news that he had rejected Allah. Neighbors then turned against him too.

"If you do not go to the mosque and publicly recant your Jesus," one declared, "we will throw you out of your home. You are not welcome here if you are not of Allah."

Again, Christians came to Musa's aid. "Come with us," they told him. "We have a safe place for you and your family to live."

So the family loaded their possessions into the back of a pickup truck and left their home behind.

"I felt blessed when this happened to me," Musa said. At the truth-or-lie crossroads, he had dared to choose Jesus. He had counted the cost and put everything at risk when he answered, "Yes, I am a follower of Christ."

The decision to follow Christ changes us and opens us up to experience the joy of the Lord. It is why the apostle Paul could experience joy and freedom even as his persecution intensified. "From now on let no one cause me trouble," he wrote, "for I bear on my body the marks of Jesus" (Galatians 6:17).

Daily, our persecuted brothers and sisters in the faith bear the marks of the Lord Jesus. They consider it a joy to remain true to him, regardless of the cost. Like Musa, they stand strong in their convictions and true to God's Word. "When the persecution came," Musa said, "my faith was tested, and I learned much more to trust the Lord."

Such is the power of joy.

How does Musa's story inspire you to pursue a life of joy in Christ that comes through obedience to him?

21

CHOOSING JOY OVER BITTERNESS

Gulnaz
Pakistan

Gulnaz, a young married Christian woman, was working at a phone center when a Muslim man came in to make a call. But then he refused to leave. When the man made sexual advances toward Gulnaz, she slapped him, and he vowed he would make her pay for her "disrespect."

Unfortunately, young Christian women in Pakistan often drink from a very bitter cup of suffering. Some men take pleasure in exerting power over these women for their own shameful satisfaction. They treat them as nothing more than possessions to be used and discarded.

Gulnaz suffered such abuse. Her would-be attacker returned and poured acid on her, badly burning her face, chest, and arms. But her story of faith and joy would not go untold. Christian medical personnel helped to provide treatment for her injuries, including surgery that enabled greater use of her severely damaged arm.

As she slowly healed from her wounds, Gulnaz experienced renewal and growth in her spiritual life as well. Instead of dwelling on her attack and the terrible scarring that resulted, Gulnaz and her husband kept their eyes firmly fixed on God. They refused to allow their circumstances to weigh them down in bitterness. Out of her tragedy emerged a triumph of God-breathed love and joy over hate.

Gulnaz and her husband live in a rundown neighborhood with open sewage in the streets and garbage piled everywhere. Looking at the needs around her, Gulnaz began witnessing to young girls. She even started a small Bible study for them.

When Christians gave Gulnaz and her husband a home in a much nicer area, the couple instead gave the keys to a Pakistani evangelist who was forced to live on the run after radical Muslims targeted his ministry. The spouses knew the home would be far more comfortable than where they lived, or they could have sold it for money they needed. But they decided the evangelist needed the home more than they did.

Their generosity and joy in the wake of the pain they endure are an inspiration to those who face even the slightest persecution.

In situations such as Gulnaz's, it is easy to allow the circumstances or the people who try to control us to define us. But if we are followers of

Christ, our approval comes from him alone. Romans 10:11 reminds us, "Everyone who believes in him will not be put to shame." Jesus loves us unconditionally, and by focusing on him rather than our circumstances, we can walk through persecution with joy and hope.

However, not one of us can stand firm in our own strength. Paul wrote, "Finally, be strong in the Lord and in the strength of his might. Put on the whole armor of God, that you may be able to stand against the schemes of the devil. For we do not wrestle against flesh and blood, but against the rulers, against the authorities, against the cosmic powers over this present darkness, against the spiritual forces of evil in the heavenly places" (Ephesians 6:10–12).

"Pray for me," is the first request front-line workers receive from our persecuted brothers and sisters in the global body of Christ. Let us pray that they not only stand firm in their faith, but they also stand tall in the joy of Jesus' love for them. Continue to pray for their physical protection as well as their spiritual protection in the battles they fight. And pray that the joy of their relationship with Christ will have an impact on those who persecute and demean them.

22

AN UNEXPLAINABLE ESCAPE

Farid
Afghanistan

At 5:00 a.m., a handful of bearded men—heads wrapped in white or beige turbans—sat in the apartment in a circle as if gathered around a campfire. What drew them together this early in the day? Not the warmth of a fire, but the light of God's Word.

Positioned on the floor in the middle of their circle, like the hub of a wheel, were hand-sketched illustrations of Bible stories. Nearby, a turquoise pitcher of water and matching basin had been prepared for foot washing.

This was a Bible study.

Speaking just above a whisper, Farid, the group leader, prayed, "We thank you, God, for your willingness to meet with us this morning. We thank you for your presence here among us."

Outside the apartment, Afghanistan's harsh and rugged landscape awakened with first light. The city's buildings blended in with the steep, rising mountains beyond, all colored in sandy shades of brown. It was difficult to tell where humanity ended and nature began.

Farid had just introduced the book of Acts when someone pounded on the door. Before anyone could react, dark-clothed intruders burst in brandishing rifles and knives. Farid was slammed to the floor. His hands were tied behind his back, a knife placed just inches from his neck. None of the six men resisted.

Amid the panic and confusion came clarity in prayer. "God," Farid prayed, "if this is the time for me to die, I forgive these people who want to kill me."

Farid believed it was an honor to give his life for God's glory. If he died, he didn't want the intruders' blood on his hands. "I wanted God to forgive them, and I wanted them to come to Christ as a result of my death," he said.

He closed his eyes, waiting for the end. When nothing happened, he sensed God wanting him to stand up and leave the room. So he stood. His hands were no longer tied. The straps simply fell to the floor. He walked toward the door, which was guarded by two armed men.

"Sit down, dog," one commanded. "You're not leaving—alive."

The other pointed his AK-47 rifle at Farid and squeezed the trigger.

Click. Nothing. The rifle had jammed.

Click. Again.

The rifle's failure to fire diverted both guards' attention, and Farid fled. As he raced down the stairs, three or four steps at a time, he heard gunfire. He saw bullets chip the wall beyond him, but he escaped unharmed.

What's even more amazing is that not one of his five companions was injured. Only the leader of the terrorist group was hurt when he was shot accidentally. The police made a chilling discovery when they arrived: inside a bag they found an al-Qaida flag, two swords, and a video camera.

According to the authorities, the terrorists had planned to film the beheading of all six men and broadcast it. Evidently, the attackers knew Farid was winning Afghan Muslims to Christ. The footage would warn missionaries, evangelists, and former Muslims that they would be killed if they didn't stop their evangelism and discipleship.

"This is a Muslim country, and men fighting for Islam have issued these threats for twenty-five years," Farid explained. As Christians in Afghanistan know all too well, "they don't like non-Muslim people coming in to preach. In the Quran, it is written that if somebody rejects Islam, you must kill them."

What terrorists wanted to accomplish that morning did not happen. The only casualty was one of their own.

The followers of Christ experienced yet another reason to rejoice in the awesome power of their sovereign God.

No wonder the apostle Paul rejoiced in his suffering and wrote of his desire to "know him (Jesus) and the power of his resurrection, and may share his sufferings, becoming like him in his death" (Philippians 3:10).

The power of the resurrection gives all Christ-followers reason for great joy. That power is at work in the lives of every Christian who walks in obedience with him, knowing they risk persecution and suffering as his witnesses. What a gift to know and believe that our God is without limits, and that he is in control of everything that happens to us!

23

FORWARD, ALWAYS FORWARD

Ishaku Manawa
Nigeria

Ishaku Manawa was riding his motorcycle on a narrow dirt road to the distant village of Ngowoshe to share the gospel. All of a sudden, he saw members of Boko Haram, a militant Islamic group, burning houses and firing rifle rounds into the air. Ishaku faced two choices: he could either turn around, hoping to avoid an encounter, or he could stay the course. But if he risked moving forward and was recognized…

Ishaku shifted gears and wound his way past the frenzied terrorists. Even though a bullet or a machete could knock him from his bike and end his life, still he rode on.

The militants glanced at Ishaku as he passed—but did nothing.

Northeastern Nigeria has long been a dangerous place for Christians. During Boko Haram's reign of terror, entire swaths of this area were under Islamic control. The two largest cities, Mubi and Yola, were once essentially ruled by Boko Haram until Nigerian government forces liberated them.

Yet the violence continues. Boko Haram struggles to regain power, and Islamic militants attack Christian villages with impunity. In one twelve-month period, nearly two hundred people were killed and another two hundred thousand displaced.

Those dire numbers are precisely why Ishaku ministers in this area. He's eager to carry the gospel where it's most desperately needed.

Ishaku and his family—a wife and seven children—live in Mubi, but each week Ishaku fires up his motorbike to visit rural villages. He knows his life is in jeopardy.

Boko Haram has killed more than fifty people under his pastoral care over the years, including thirty-seven from a single congregation. While Ishaku has grieved their loss, his grief is tempered knowing that they were people of strong faith. "There are others whose deaths troubled me," he said, "because they weren't as strong as they should have been." Those losses impel him to continue teaching and strengthening the faith of his flock—preparing them to face whatever persecution they may encounter because they know Christ.

And he moves forward, always forward.

Ishaku smiled as he recalled how even some former Boko Haram radicals have placed their faith in Jesus Christ. One seventeen-year-old girl, who once attacked Christians, became a Christ-follower. To both protect and disciple her, Ishaku arranged for her to move in with a Christian woman in another part of Nigeria.

And then there's Shuaibu. He'd zealously persecuted Christians until the day he heard street preachers calling on their congregations to pray for those who were killing them. Hearing Christians speak of their attackers with compassion stopped Shuaibu in his tracks—and led to him declaring his faith in Jesus Christ.

Ishaku has adapted his ministry to the shifting situation in Nigeria. When hundreds of thousands of Nigerians were displaced by Boko Haram, he planted a church in a large refugee camp just across the border in Cameroon. And he provided food and comfort to local farmers who were attacked and run out of their villages by militants. He does what he can to meet believers' physical needs and encourages them to continue following Christ.

He makes sure they have a place to gather and worship—whether in a building, a tent, under a tree, or even beneath the open sky.

Moving his flock forward, always forward.

Ishaku's ministry has required him to be away from home often. His wife is fully aware the time may come when her husband's ministry costs him his life, but she has encouraged him to continue serving. She squeezes his hand, and tells him if he hears of people who need to hear God's Word, he should go and share it.

She knows her husband well: Ishaku wouldn't be content to sit on the sidelines in safety. He's called to go out among the suffering believers who need the support and teaching he can offer.

Ishaku's children pray for him often, and his eldest daughter occasionally accompanies him on ministry trips. They have all been taught that suffering and sacrifice come with following Christ.

But so does joy.

Especially when faith and ministry are moving forward—always forward.

Ishaku would be surprised to discover many believers are inspired by his faithful commitment to carry the gospel forward. For him, it's nothing special—it's simply part of following Jesus and doing what God calls every believer to do.

Hebrews 12:1–2 reinforces Ishaku's dedication: "Therefore, since we are surrounded by so great a cloud of witnesses, let us lay aside every weight, and sin which clings so closely, and let us run with endurance the race that is set before us, looking to Jesus, the founder and perfecter of our faith, who for the joy that was set before him endured the cross, despising the shame, and is seated at the right hand of the throne of God."

Serving faithfully is where Christians find peace and fulfillment. It is where they walk most closely with Christ.

And where they find joy.

24

NO LONGER ON
THE SIDELINES

Akhom and Hassani
Egypt

The old men who usually gathered at the corner cafés each night to smoke *shisha* and play board games were absent. In their place, hundreds of Egyptian Christians walked peacefully through the streets of the Coptic neighborhood of Mokattam.

Since the January 2011 revolution that led to more than eight hundred people being killed and more than six thousand injured, Egypt had been awash in social, political, and cultural turmoil. Everywhere, it seemed, individuals were standing up for what they believed—or standing up to silence the beliefs of others.

The demonstration in Mokattam marked the end of forty days of mourning following sectarian clashes that killed twenty-seven people, most of them Christians. Marchers boldly identified themselves as Christ-followers in this predominantly Muslim country.

By standing together, they were making a powerful statement to the world—regardless of the cost.

The Christian community in Egypt had been under repeated attack since the revolution began—by both the Egyptian military and Muslim extremists. Two cousins living in Mokattam were severely injured during an assault on March 8, 2011.

Twenty-one-year-old Akhom considered himself a Christian but knew his spiritual life was lacking—it was more "going through the motions" than a serious commitment. But one turbulent night changed all that.

Attackers started throwing rocks, bricks, and broken glass from a six-story apartment building. Clashes broke out. Suddenly, a man fired three shots into Akhom's face and one into his stomach. His cousin Hassani was also injured when an attacker cut his face with a machete.

Both men survived, which some consider a miracle. But the cousins recognized an even greater miracle as they healed in the hospital. The brutal attack and the horrible wounds they suffered led them to fully commit their lives to Jesus Christ.

Akhom's shattered jaw had to be stabilized and anchored with screws; his stomach was scarred from the bullet and the incisions to retrieve it. But the destruction of his body led to a renewal of his spirit.

"The attack helped me to get closer to God," he said. "I was away from the Lord. I was doing bad things, living a life of sin. While I was healing, I was always asking the Lord to change me, to make more perfection in my heart."

The pain he suffered wasn't without meaning; it was pain infused with the joy of a more intimate relationship with Jesus.

"Persecution is part of our faith," Akhom said. Referring to the life of Jesus, he explained, "He was persecuted, and he told us in the world we would suffer. But he made sure we knew he overcame the world, so we are following the same model. We have to rejoice in what the Bible tells us. If persecution happens in our life, then it is a privilege to us. It means we are going the right way. We couldn't see it before, but now I see our trials the Lord allowed us to have. This is strengthening our faith."

Hassani experienced a similar transformation. His injuries required months of painful reconstructive surgery on his face, but even more significant was the transformation of his heart.

"Before the attack, I did not have any time to be with the Lord to pray," he recalled. "God was not there in my life. I did not know him as a Good Shepherd. But a new vision came after the attack. My heart was opened to realize the grace of the Lord. I now see him as a Good Shepherd because it is a miracle I am alive!"

With joy, he thanks God for the prayers and medical assistance that Christians provided during his time of need.

"It is exactly as the Bible says," Hassani continued. "I can never forget the blessing God sent to me. Because of him, I'm alive. He showed me mercy."

No longer playing it "safe," no longer experiencing the emptiness of a halfhearted commitment to Jesus, Hassani and Akhom choose to trust in Jesus and stand for him in a country where his message is not welcome. They walk in the confidence of 2 Timothy 1:7: "For God gave us a spirit not of fear but of power and love and self-control."

Armed with the power of God's love and filled with the joy of knowing Jesus, Hassani spoke for both of them when he said, "We are praying for those persecutors who are killing us, that they may know the truth. I feel sorry for them and for those who are far from the Lord. They are really suffering."

Join Hassani in praying for his persecutors. And pray for those who oppose your witness for Christ.

25

2.6 MILLION ...AND ONE

Brahim
Niger

Brahim scarcely noticed when a group of strangers walked past his prison cell. With the temperature hovering at nearly 120 degrees, he didn't have the energy to be curious.

For three years he'd sweltered in this hotbox of a prison sitting in the brutal Sahara desert sun. Relentless heat had killed some prisoners, driven others nearly insane. Brahim was still hanging on—but for how long?

Then he realized the visitors hadn't come to gawk or lecture about Islam, but rather to install ceiling fans and scrub clean the filthy bathrooms. Windows they put in place now kept the oppressive winds from scorching his cell.

They even brought a television for the prisoners.

These men didn't work for the prison or government. They'd come to help Brahim and other prisoners not out of obligation, but because they loved Jesus Christ.

Brahim took notice of their actions. *Before they even opened their mouths to preach,* he thought, *these actions of taking care of people who were desperate and in terrible conditions are turning my heart toward Christianity.*

A few of the visitors returned each Sunday to read from the Bible and share the gospel with prisoners. Brahim had committed a crime, but these men didn't seem to care. Their message of grace and forgiveness was one the inmate desperately needed to hear. Brahim also knew they were practicing what they were teaching. *I can see that this group of people fears God,* he thought. That gave him the confirmation he needed that they were on the right path, and he eventually placed his trust in Jesus Christ.

Brahim studied the Bible he was given and watched the *JESUS* film provided by his new Christian friends.

And when he was released, he met with a pastor to deepen his understanding of God's Word. He wanted to be ready to discuss his new faith with his family when he got home.

Once he'd settled in, Brahim felt God calling him to take the gospel to other Tuareg, a people group living in his region of Niger as well as several other countries, including Algeria, Burkina Faso, Libya, and Mali. But he didn't want just some of his Tuareg tribe to place their trust in Christ—he wanted all of them to follow Christ.

All 2.6 million of them.

"The objective is to take the gospel to everybody, not just a few," Brahim said.

Compounding his challenge was the semi-nomadic lifestyle of the Tuareg, who travel with their livestock on a seasonal basis. Though they occasionally spend time on designated farmland, most of the year they range across the Sahara.

Brahim's mission field was literally a moving target.

Yet the joy he found in Christ fueled an urgency to share that joy. He prayerfully set a goal to accomplish his mission within seven years, no matter the cost.

Brahim started with his family. He first led his wife and seven adult children to Christ, then shared the Good News with other relatives, most of whom immediately decided to follow Jesus.

His next move was strategic. Brahim met with his tribe's regional leader to discuss his plan for witnessing to the Tuareg people. The elder listened and nodded thoughtfully. "I am not Christian, but I am not against Christians," the leader told Brahim. "Whoever wants to become Christian in these more than one hundred villages, he is free."

That's all Brahim needed to hear.

With help from the pastor who had discipled him, Brahim gathered together hundreds of people in his clan. He then stood and quieted the crowd as he began to share the gospel.

The joy he felt shone brightly. "The truth I discovered is about Jesus," he told the crowd. "He is the way. He is the light. Whoever does not follow him cannot meet God.

"Now, who would like to put their trust in Christ? Please raise your hand."

More than four hundred hands shot up.

The pastor carefully recorded the name of each convert.

"I want it to be public so many people in the village will know you are a Christian," he told them.

Brahim promised the new believers he'd return to share more about Jesus Christ and the Bible.

Two of Brahim's family members soon joined him in his ministry work—his adult son, Wararni, and his cousin, Usaden, who serves as chief of his village. Like Brahim, they both strongly desired to share the gospel with the Tuaregs.

Their approach to evangelism is simple. When they visit a village, they look for a "man of peace," someone kindhearted, trusted by his community, and open to hearing the gospel. When that man gives himself to Jesus Christ, he in turn shares the gospel with his people. Then, one or two of the evangelists who led Brahim to the Lord visit to read stories from the Bible and answer questions.

Since the three evangelists launched their ministry, between one hundred and one thousand people have come to faith each time they preach. There's a strong family and tribal connection among the Tuareg. When villagers see their leader embrace something, they're open to it as well. So the evangelists focus on converting tribal leaders, leveraging those influencers when approaching others.

While seeing large numbers of new believers is exciting, Brahim and his team also take discipleship seriously. They want every convert to be taught and discipled so their new faith grows—and they're prepared to share it. The support of other believers is essential.

Brahim has established nineteen churches and Usaden has started six. Wararni and his wife have founded eight churches. The Tuareg believers who have spiritual homes are thriving.

Is there joy in this journey of sharing Christ? Absolutely, though there are challenges as well.

Brahim laughed as he described the necessary preparations so a new believer can make a public profession of faith. In order to baptize in the Sahara, he has to dig a hole, line it with the tarp he always carries, and then find enough water to fill it up.

Local Islamic leaders were livid when they heard that hundreds of people in multiple villages were coming to Christ. At one point, a group of men appeared at Brahim's house to warn him: if he didn't stop his ministry work, they'd kill him and his family.

Brahim wasn't intimidated. "I know if you touch me, you are declaring war with heaven," he replied.

They left without incident.

Wararni has also faced persecution. He nearly lost his life when two Fulani chiefs and two Tuareg chiefs told a local government official that Wararni and his wife were forcing people to leave Islam.

Such accusations aren't uncommon and normally amount to nothing because the Nigerien constitution guarantees religious freedom. But this time the chiefs decided to take matters into their own hands.

Wararni and a friend were chatting on the street when the four Muslims silently surrounded the pair. The chiefs each carried a sword, and one held a pistol.

"What are you doing here?" Wararni's friend asked.

"We are after him," one of the Muslims replied, pointing to Wararni.

This is the day they will end my life, thought Wararni, *but I am so happy, even if they kill me as I do this work.* Although Wararni was prepared to die for Christ at that moment, he also wanted to continue serving him.

As his friend argued with the assassins, Wararni quickly phoned a friend who served in the military.

Within minutes, a jeep carrying his friend and three additional soldiers screeched to a halt beside the group of men. "There are four bandits here who want to attack us!" Wararni told them.

The four assailants were quickly shoved into the vehicle and hauled away.

The persecution Brahim and his team encounter isn't a surprise, nor does it lessen their joy in serving Christ. Persecution is a part of their lives. "And it is a part of the life of many of my disciples," Wararni noted. "They expect it."

As Brahim reflects on what's happened among the Tuareg and Fulani tribes—and how proud he is of the faithful work of his team—he can't help but be joyful. "I am so happy, more than how somebody can be happy," he said. "Whatever problem I face, or I am facing, when I think of what is happening, I forget about everything. I just rejoice in the Lord."

But he is not satisfied. There are still many among that 2.6 million who have yet to hear about Jesus.

And Brahim is all too happy to tell them.

Brahim isn't crazy. He knows reaching 2.6 million people in just a few years is a lofty goal. But he also knows it's God's will that all people—every person on the planet—hear the gospel. In fact, God "desires all people to be saved and to come to the knowledge of the truth" (1 Timothy 2:4).

All people!

Even if Brahim doesn't hit his goal, he's exactly in the center of God's will, doing just what God has asked him to do.

And there's no more joyful place to be than cooperating with God's purposes.

If you'd like more joy in your life, start there. Ask God what he's doing in your corner of the world and commit to being part of it.

You may have to dig a few holes in the desert, but that's where you'll find joy.

QUESTIONS FOR REFLECTION AND DISCUSSION

JOY

1. A.W. Tozer wrote: "...the people of God ought to be the happiest people in all the wide world! People should be coming to us constantly and asking the source of our joy and delight..."[1]

   a. Why would Tozer believe that the people of God ought to be the happiest, most joyful people in the whole wide world? What is the source of joy for Christians? Why do you think that?

   b. Is joy different from happiness? How so?

   c. Who is the most joyful person you know? What do you notice about their attitudes and actions that lead you to believe they are joyful?

---

1. Tozer, A. W. *Who Put Jesus on the Cross?* (Camp Hill, PA: Wingspread Publishers, 2009), p. 134.

2. Read Luke 6:22–23. Joy is probably not the first expression we associate with persecuted followers of Jesus. They may be tortured, abused, and imprisoned. They may have friends and family members who have been killed for their faith. They may be forced to flee their homes, leaving behind everything they own. Yet joy is often what people notice most when they encounter these believers.

   a. Why are those who suffer filled to overflowing with joy?

   b. How did Jon from Malaysia demonstrate his joy in Christ?

   c. What did Musa of North Africa do to show that his joy was not based on his circumstance of suffering but came from his relationship with Christ?

   d. When your life is pressed by difficult circumstances, how would those closest to you describe your responses? How can you be inspired by the stories of people like Jon and Musa to choose joy?

3. Though Gulnaz experienced pain and scarring from the acid burns as she was violently assaulted by her Muslim assailant, she and her husband's joy and hope thrived as they fixed their eyes on God.

   a. Read John 15:11. For Christians, true joy lies far beyond the security, ease, and comfort of this world. It lies far beyond the way that people treat us in this life. Our joyful hope has as its source something more powerful than anything else in this world.

b. What does "that my joy may be in you" mean? How are you encouraged knowing that the source of joy, for the biblical disciple, is Christ? What ways did Christ demonstrate joy during his earthly life?

c. What has Christ spoken to you about that resulted in overflowing joy? How does having a life full of joy give you an ability to overcome negative circumstances or opposition? How does having a life full of joy give you the ability to live fruitfully for Christ?

4. Planting nineteen churches and discipling hundreds of Christian converts is a joyful part of Brahim's ministry in Niger. It is easy to relate to the joy he experiences as he faithfully advances the gospel against the forces of spiritual darkness. But he was also joyful when hundreds of angry Muslims threatened him and his family because of their faith.

a. Read James 1:2.

b. What does it mean when James writes to encourage the early church (and us) to "count it all joy"? Think about the followers of Christ in the stories you just read. How do they show that they have counted persecution, threats, and opposition as joy?

c. What might it look like for you to count, as joy, a difficult season you are experiencing?

i.   What would a joyful attitude display to others?

ii. What would joyful words sound like?

iii. What would joyful actions look like?

iv. What commitment are you willing to make to be
     more joyful in your attitude, words, and actions this
     week in order to demonstrate your faith in Christ?

Pray

Ask God to give our persecuted brothers and sisters like Brahim a
joy that is complete in Christ Jesus our Lord. Pray for your own
measure of joy to demonstrate to a lost world your faith in Christ.

Part IV

PERSEVERANCE

*And you will be hated by all for my name's sake. But
the one who endures to the end will be saved.*

MARK 13:13

From beginning to end, the Bible is full of promises for those who
faithfully seek to know and serve the living God. We often look to
such promises for encouragement when we encounter difficulties
in life, particularly when we face challenges in our walk with God.
But take a look at Christ's promise in John 15:20: "Remember the
word that I said to you: 'A servant is not greater than his master.' If
they persecuted me, they will also persecute you. If they kept my
word, they will also keep yours." And Mark 13:13: "And you will
be hated by all for my name's sake. But the one who endures to the
end will be saved."

What promises! The certainty of persecution isn't the kind of
encouragement most of us hope to find in God's Word. But if
persecution is a reality for all who live in obedience to Christ, then
we certainly need encouragement. We need to learn how to endure

to the end. To persevere as a follower of Christ means to stand firm and resist whatever opposition rises against us. The picture that comes to mind is that of a person who leans into and stands against a strong wind or plants his feet and pushes back against a powerful river current.

Persecuted Christians learn quickly that it is impossible to persevere in their own strength. Jesus knew it would be that way. During the last Passover meal he shared with his disciples, he talked about how necessary it would be for them to remain in a life-giving relationship with him. He said bluntly, "As the branch cannot bear fruit by itself, unless it abides in the vine, neither can you, unless you abide in me. I am the vine; you are the branches… apart from me you can do nothing" (John 15:4–5).

Think about that last phrase once more: "Apart from me you can do *nothing*" (emphasis added). Absolutely nothing.

If we want to be Christ-followers who stand firm as we serve him, we, too, must abide in him. We must be rooted in the character and Word of God. We must cling to our relationship with him, growing closer to him, experiencing more of who he is, and discovering what it means to walk with him in faith. Day by day, as our intimacy with God grows, his strength empowers us to obey and endure faithfully, regardless of the cost.

David had a heart that earnestly pursued a relationship with God. In Psalm 40:1–2, he wrote about the strength that relationship provided in the face of pain and adversity: "I waited patiently for the LORD; he inclined to me and heard my cry. He…set my feet upon a rock, making my steps secure."

Joseph spent many years enslaved and imprisoned. Despite the suffering he endured at the hands of people who mistreated him, lied about him, and forgot about him, God was with him (Genesis 39:2). Rather than removing Joseph from his suffering, God empowered him to stand firm, to learn to trust and obey him in everything. Later, Joseph played an important role as God unfolded his plans and purposes in establishing the ancient nation of Israel.

Every day in countries where Islamic extremists exert control, followers of Christ stand firm in their commitment to trust God and obediently fulfill his purpose for their lives. They pay a high personal price for persevering in their faith. They endure fierce hostility, brutal cruelty, and unthinkable atrocities, yet they remain true to God. As you read their stories, notice how the strength of their relationship with their Lord and Savior empowers them to "run with endurance the race" that is set before them (Hebrews 12:1).

26

CALLED TO SERVE— EVEN WHEN DISPLACED

Pastors Armando, Matateu, and Carlos
Mozambique

As cries of *"Allahu Akbar!"* (Allah is great!) pierced the spring night, Pastor Armando and his family fled their home. Villagers scrambled in every direction, frantically attempting to find safety. Many took cover in the bush as Islamic insurgents set fire to homes and killed anyone in sight.

In the chaos, Pastor Armando lost track of his four-year-old and seven-year-old children.

Days later, when he could finally return to search for them, the charred rubble of former homes and churches—and the decapitated bodies of many villagers, including children—were all that remained.

"Jesus said, 'Take care of my sheep,'" Pastor Armando said through tears. "But my sheep are scattered, and I don't know how to find them." He still doesn't know what became of his children.

On another day that spring, Islamists gathered everyone in Pastor Matateu's village, then asked each person one question: "What is your religion?"

Those who answered "Christian" were shoved to their knees and beheaded. Pastors were tortured and then murdered, as were their wives and children.

In all, seventy villagers were killed in the attack. Survivors say that following the slaughter, the insurgents raised an Islamic flag and declared the establishment of sharia, or Islamic law.

Pastor Matateu and his family, who had escaped into the bush, survived there for more than a month before finally being rescued by sympathetic friends.

And Pastor Carlos will never forget the sight of burned cars containing the scorched bodies of those who tried driving to safety during an especially horrific Islamist attack on his village.

Not only Christians were killed but also nominal Muslims unable to recite specific Islamic creeds. The ambush left mountains of bodies in the village's bloodied streets. "We felt like chickens going into a lion's den," Pastor Carlos lamented.

In Cabo Delgado, Mozambique's northernmost province bordering Tanzania, Muslims are coming to faith in Christ, and Christians are moving into the region to find work. Insurgents, who pledge allegiance to the self-proclaimed Islamic State (ISIS) in Africa, have intensified their raids with the influx of believers.

These Islamic radicals, known as Ahl al-Sunnah wal-Jamaah ("adherents of the prophetic tradition"), are remnants of an extremist group from Tanzania. They began targeting Christian villages in the region, overrunning entire towns.

The media often attributes attacks to the terrorists' desire to control oil and natural gas fields. But another, darker motive is also at work: creating an Islamic caliphate (Islamic state) in northern Mozambique.

The ongoing assaults have resulted in uprooting some 800,000 Christians and cultural Muslims who now live in camps for internally displaced persons (IDP). And after being abused by Islam, many Muslims are more receptive to God's message of love and grace expressed in Jesus Christ.

Armando, Matateu, Carlos, and thousands of other Christians persevere in sharing their faith. Even as they struggle with the horrors they witnessed and the losses they endured, the pastors continue serving others in the IDP camps as they preach, teach, and distribute food to the hungry.

They persevere because of their unshakable confidence in God. In spite of the endless rows of tents and sea of misery that surround them, the three men trust that God is in control and hasn't abandoned them.

"The reason I keep going and serving is because I have confidence in God," Pastor Armando said. "I have no belief in anything else. I trust in him alone. This calling that is on my life is to serve, so if I leave now in the middle of all this, who will be left to serve these people? So of course, I will continue to do so."

They persevere because they have faith in the one true God.

When asked about his commitment to continue his ministry amid the suffering he's experienced, Pastor Matateu boldly proclaimed, "What could separate me from God? Death, no! The war, no! So of course, I will continue to serve my God." While Christians are displaced by Islamists in their country, they know they are not displaced from God's love.

His words echo the apostle Paul's in Romans 8:35, 37–39: "Who shall separate us from the love of Christ? Shall tribulation, or distress, or persecution, or family, or nakedness, or danger, or sword?...No, in all these things we are more than conquerors through him who loved us. For I am sure that neither death nor life, nor angels nor rulers, nor things present nor things to come, nor powers, nor height nor depth, nor anything else in all creation, will be able to separate us from the love of God in Christ Jesus our Lord."

When we face trials, we can persevere in obedience like Pastor Matateu because we can have the same unshakeable confidence he has: nothing can separate us from the love of Christ. Pray that, like Armando, Matateu, and Carlos, you can boldly obey God and serve him each day, no matter the cost, because of his great love for you.

27

THE BOY WHO WOULD NOT BACK DOWN

Hussein B.
Turkey

At his school in Turkey, nine-year-old Hussein fumbled excitedly with the clasp on his chain. After fastening it around his neck, he straightened the cross pendant. He was proud to let his teachers and fellow students know of his new Christian faith.

The feeling would not be mutual.

Hussein was unaware that 96 percent of Turks are Muslim. Although many do not practice their faith, most believe that all Turks should be Muslim. He didn't know that believing in a different religion is culturally unacceptable. And he didn't know that despite government claims of religious tolerance, Christians are not welcome in many parts of his country.

Hussein, in his innocence, put on the cross that morning not knowing it would incite danger. He knew only that his father, a former Islamic scholar, loved Jesus and so did he. His faith was as real to him as the cross he'd just placed around his neck.

"I felt so alive hearing the hymns and singing in the church," he said, describing his first time attending a service. "I felt I had to learn more about this. I was so joyful, and I thought this might be my last time in church. So I opened the hymnal and thought about tearing the pages out and keeping them. I did not take them, but I wanted to so badly."

A year after that experience, Hussein wore his cross to school, in part because he thought it could be a good way to talk with other students about his faith. "It's not the physical cross; it's the meaning of the cross," the precocious boy explained. "It is a beautiful thing. I wanted people to ask me about it so I could tell them about Christ."

But he was not prepared for their reaction. Some students spit on the cross. Others swore at him. "Stinkin' kafir," they called out. They threatened him because he embraced the dreaded "religion of the West."

One of his sisters told their parents about the cross. "Hussein is telling everyone that we are Christians!"

Hakeem, his father, bristled. "Don't *ever* tell people that you have become a Christian," he warned. "You don't want to get us into trouble. You must not wear that to school again!"

Later, Hakeem and his wife decided they had been wrong to force their son to suppress his faith. The couple realized they had suppressed *their* faith and that Hussein's boldness, naive and idealistic as it was, should be celebrated, not condemned.

"We were trying to prevent conflicts with others, but we came to the realization that we were the ones with a problem," Hakeem said. "We decided to be like Hussein, more open about our Christianity."

Although his parents now supported Hussein's desire to tell others about his faith, his classmates continued to taunt him. He threatened to go to the principal if the abuse didn't stop. One boy grabbed him by the arm, squeezed his hand hard, and warned, "I'm going to *shoot you* if you tell about this."

After Hussein described this incident, Hakeem went to the other boy's father. "I thought the father would be concerned about his son's actions," Hakeem said. "But instead, he called me a kafir, threatened me, and said he would shoot me himself if I pursued action against his son."

So the persecution continued. A gang of boys jumped Hussein, threw rocks at him, and beat him with sticks. He screamed in pain as a classmate dragged him along the ground by his shirt. The attack stopped only when Hakeem arrived to pick up his son.

The opposition to Hussein's faith grew even stronger. When Hakeem asked his son if he was still getting beaten up, the boy nodded.

"By whom?" his father asked.

"By my religion teacher," Hussein replied.

His religion teacher was an imam, an Islamic leader, who led worship in the neighborhood mosque. Every student in his class was required to write and recite the *shahada*[1]: "There is no god but Allah, and Muhammad is his prophet."

Hussein refused. In response, the teacher repeatedly struck him with a wooden rod. The boy continued to endure beatings each time he rejected the shahada.

"It isn't in my heart," Hussein said. "It's just meaningless words to me."

After three weeks of such beatings, Hussein had a seizure. Then another. And another. When Hakeem went to the school to confront the teacher, he found the man standing over Hussein, holding the rod.

The teacher stared at Hakeem. "Are you aware," he stated icily, "that your son is wearing a cross to school? Are you Christians?"

"Yes and yes," Hakeem replied.

"It is against Islam!" the teacher declared.

"Why are you punishing my son for not reciting a Muslim prayer?" Hakeem asked. "Are beatings permissible?"

"Yes," the teacher said, "the principal and the parents agree I should." Hakeem and his wife transferred their son to another school, and then another before they found one where Hussein experienced fewer attacks.

"I will never return to Islam, even if the persecution continues," *Hussein said. "Christ said we would suffer for him. It's okay to suffer*

---

1. The shahada is the Islamic profession of faith.

for Christ, and we should be happy to suffer for him. The Lord is with me."

Even at a young age, Hussein knew his goal was not to please man but to please God. *"And I tell you, everyone who acknowledges me before men,"* Jesus taught, *"the Son of Man also will acknowledge before the angels of God, but the one who denies me before men will be denied before the angels of God"* (Luke 12:8–9).

Let us not forget our brothers and sisters—even children such as Hussein—who are persecuted for standing firm in their faith, yet persevere. Will we stand with them in their suffering? Will we persevere with them in our prayers and in providing support for them? How does Hussein's story inspire you to persevere?

28

A MODERN-DAY JOB

John
Nigeria

In the village of Maseh in Nigeria's Plateau State, where farmland and gardens separate thatch-roof dwellings, Pastor John Ali Doro awoke and began preparing for the day. His busy lifestyle required him to wear several different hats. He was leader of a small but committed group of Christians. He was husband to a woman he loved. He was father to seven children and grandfather to a handful of boys and girls.

Life was good, but no pastor in Nigeria assumes such a role without accepting risk. Christians are the minority among the predominantly Muslim Fulani, an ethnic group that raises cattle in the region. Militant Fulani Muslims have increasingly become more violent in their attacks against Christians. John was well aware that radical Islamic groups had already killed dozens of pastors.

Gunfire suddenly shattered the morning peace, followed by shouts of terror. "The Fulani are coming!" someone yelled.

Pastor John dived into a nearby ditch to hide from the armed militants. From a distance, he saw the Fulani militants zeroing in on his church. It was the largest building in the village, and people had run into it for safety. Flames soon burst through the windows. Helpless, Pastor John watched and listened in agony as dozens of his brothers and sisters in Christ—some members of his own family—wailed as they burned to death.

"Allahu akbar! Allahu akbar!" (Allah is great!), shouted the Fulani militants.

Then Pastor John heard one say, "Let's see if their God can save them now!"

After Nigerian Special Forces finally drove the attackers away, the smell of charred human flesh proved a prelude to the painful revelation inside. Forty-four people lay dead, including Pastor John's wife, four of his seven children, and two of his grandchildren.

But the killing wasn't over.

The next day, at a mass funeral for those who died, the gunmen returned. They opened fire on the mourners. Among those killed were a national senator and a leader of the Plateau State House of Assembly. John learned that around ten other villages had been similarly attacked the previous day, leaving nearly two hundred people dead.

The common thread in the attacks? The targets were Christians.

At home, Pastor John tried unsuccessfully to make sense of the senselessness. It was impossible. Bitterness beckoned him, and his instinct was for revenge. Instead, he made a choice.

"I just threw everything back to God," he said. "I prayed God would help the attackers understand that this is evil so that they can stop. I also asked God to help me to be able to use my life to propagate the gospel, because I knew that I could have died."

Instead of wishing evil on the extremists, he forgave the men who killed his family and friends. He hopes they will receive salvation through Jesus Christ. And although forgiveness brings healing, it does not erase sorrow and grief.

"It's painful," Pastor John said. "When they did all that and I lost my family, it was very painful. But there's nothing you can do to change the situation apart from lifting it to God." For encouragement to endure, he turned to the book of Job, the Bible's account of a man who had wave after tragic wave wash over him. "Job lost everything—wealth, children, everything but his wife," John said. "Yet he did not turn his back on God. That story has helped me, not only to deal with the situation, but even to remain who I am."

Pastor John related so closely to Job's story that he preached several sermons on it following the attack. "Job's wife told him to curse God and die," he said, "but his reply was that in the days where there is good from the Lord, we accept it. When there is difficulty, how can we refuse to accept that? Those thoughts encourage me and give me strength."

Armed with the steadfastness of God's Word, Pastor John continues to pray for church members who lost loved ones during the attack. He continues to trust God and serve him.

"My request is that God should help me in my life as a Christian and as a pastor," he said, "to be able to do what God has called me to do well, and to fulfill the purpose that God has for my life."

Adversity is unavoidable in life, but it does not necessitate defeat. The Word of God never promises a comfortable and secure life for followers of Christ. It promises that, despite the inevitable storms of life, God is bigger than such storms. "In the world you will have tribulation. But take heart; I have overcome the world" (John 16:33).

God uses perseverance to test us, steel us, and form us into the people he wants us to be. Is this process easy? No. Just as sand on a beach results from the tumult of tides and waves, our character is shaped by the pain and difficulties we have endured for Christ.

When trouble comes your way—and it will, as Pastor John knows so well—don't run from it or retaliate. Trust in God and endure in faith, so you can fulfill the purpose God has for your life.

29

IT STARTED WITH A SOCCER GAME

Hassan S. and Pastor Hakim
Algeria

In 1983, a group of Algerian locals watched tourists set up their tents in the Tizi Ouzou Province one evening. "It was a windy place, and they set up the tents the wrong way," remembered Hassan, who was there with about a dozen friends. "The wind blew everything over—their tents and their belongings. We laughed at them and then went over to help."

One of the visitors thanked them for the help and then, in the spirit of friendship, extended an unusual invitation: "Would you do us the pleasure of engaging in a friendly soccer match tomorrow?"

Hassan huddled with his friends, then replied, "We would love to, but our best player is sick in bed with a fever. Without him, we would probably not give you much of a game."

One of the visitors, his brow furrowed, asked, "This friend of yours—might we see him? We'd like to pray for his healing."

Now Hassan and his friends had furrowed brows. Prayer? Healing? God being interested in a single individual? These concepts seemed odd to the Algerians, yet they were intrigued by the offer.

So that night, the tourists prayed over the young man. In the morning, he no longer felt sick and played in the game. Amazed, the Algerians began asking questions about this apparent healing. "Who is this 'Father' you prayed to who heals?" Hassan asked.

The tourists weren't missionaries. They were simply believers who loved the Lord and were eager to share his glory. They explained the grace, salvation, and power offered through faith in Christ. The group said their goodbyes and continued on with their journey—but Algeria would not remain the same.

Algeria is an African country across the Mediterranean Sea from Spain. At one time, it was home to St. Augustine of Hippo, one of the most influential Christian scholars in history. But in more modern times, Christianity was nearly unknown. Before that soccer game, Algeria had no Christian bookstores, no functioning indigenous churches, and virtually no access to Bibles. The lone vestiges of Christian influence were abandoned churches left over from French colonialism, which ended in 1962. The few people attending church were generally foreign-born Catholics, who were allowed by law to practice their religion but forbidden to share it with the nation's Muslim population.

But after the tourists left, something "miraculous" started happening. "I felt that the stories they told were not just stories, but real," Hassan recalled. "It made me want to leave everything and follow Jesus." Hassan and other Algerians began turning to the God of the Bible. The "soccer miracle" is credited with initiating an explosion of faith in a country where Christians were once rare.

"We cannot count the number of people who came to Christ because of this," Hassan said. "We don't know how it happened, just that people came to faith and came to God."

In a short time, Christianity flourished and became the fastest-growing religion in Algeria. Pressured by hard-line Islamic nations, the Algerian government decided to curb the growth of Christianity and oppose followers of Jesus. Hassan and his friends were arrested time after time. But they and other believers would not be deterred. They remained faithful, and Christianity continued to spread.

Years, then decades, passed, and Christianity remained a "problem" for radical Muslims. So in 2006, the Algerian parliament tightened restrictions on non-Islamic organizations. The passing of Ordinance 06-03 limited Christian worship to buildings that were registered with the government. The law also restricted non-Islamic literature and set criminal penalties for anyone who "incites, constrains, or utilizes means of seduction tending to convert a Muslim to another religion" or who produces literature or videos that are designed to "shake the faith of Muslims." Violators face five years in prison and a $13,000 fine.

In keeping with this ordinance, Algerian authorities closed twenty-six churches—buildings and house churches—in February 2008, claiming they were not registered. No new churches have been given government clearance since.

But God is in the miracle business. As one Algerian pastor said, "When God says he will continue his work, he will do that. We have a lot of problems, but each time we can see God's hand in the midst of trouble."

Shortly before the restrictions of Ordinance 06-03 went into effect, local authorities had granted a pastor a permit to build a new church in northern Algeria. Pastor Hakim was elated when he received the news. By 2009, more than 300 people were coming to this church to worship—quite rare in a nation where 96 percent of the population is Muslim.

But Muslim extremists retaliated against Christians violently and forcefully. In December 2009, more than twenty Muslims blocked the church entrance and prevented people from attending a Christmas service. Two days later, protesters broke into the building and stole microphones and speakers.

The next month, Muslims burst into a church service where they intimidated the congregation and threatened to kill Pastor Hakim. A week later, demonstrators stormed the church building and vandalized it until police arrived. Later, the protesters returned and burned the building to the ground, leaving a charred mess of Bibles, hymnals, and a cross.

The Christian community would not be deterred. They rebuilt the church. Again, Muslim extremists vandalized it. Again, the followers of Jesus persisted. When they were unable to perform baptisms in their church building, they baptized believers in kiddie pools and bathtubs in congregants' homes. No matter what obstacles they face, they remain committed to obeying Jesus in whatever way possible.

The Bible reminds us that biblical disciples should expect difficulties. Accepting this, however, is not to admit defeat. As Acts 14:21–22 says, "When they [Paul and Barnabas] had preached the gospel to that city and had made many disciples, they returned to Lystra and to Iconium and to Antioch, strengthening the souls of the disciples, encouraging them to continue in the faith, and saying that through many tribulations we must enter the kingdom of God."

But in this passage, Luke, the writer of Acts, uses the word "tribulations," which means affliction, trouble, anguish, persecution. Even Paul and Barnabas knew that such tribulations had an eternal award: entering the kingdom of God.

Let that reality strengthen you as you persevere as Christ's witness no matter where you live.

30

ENEMIES IN HER OWN HOUSEHOLD

Mussalam
Uzbekistan

Mussalam, a Russian literature teacher, looked up in shock as the door of her classroom banged open. Her son, daughter, and two of her daughter's employees rushed in.

They grabbed Mussalam's arms and forcibly carried her out of the room as thirty horrified children watched.

Mussalam's heart was racing. Given all she had experienced at the hands of her grown children, her dramatic removal from the classroom was no surprise.

The abuse had started twenty years earlier when one of Mussalam's daughters placed her faith in Jesus Christ. Mussalam listened as her daughter shared the gospel, and soon she and her husband left Islam and became followers of Christ. So did Anton, one of her sons.

Mussalam's four other children remained Muslim. Her oldest daughter, Inessa, was hostile toward her mother for making such a decision. She was especially upset with Mussalam when she gave Bibles to neighbors.

Shortly after one of Mussalam's daughters unexpectedly died, her grief was interrupted by a knock on her door. Inessa had accused her mother of murdering her sister, and police were launching an investigation. Though Mussalam was cleared of any wrongdoing, Inessa continued attacking her mother.

Inessa's opposition to her mother's bold witness continued. Though Inessa owned her own home as well as a restaurant, she decided to claim her parents' home. When she announced she and two of her Muslim brothers would be moving in, Mussalam blocked the unwanted occupants. "It wouldn't be a healthy mix," she told them, thinking that would settle the matter.

It didn't.

The three Muslim siblings then took their parents to court, claiming the elderly couple was planning to use the house as a church. Mussalam's daughters-in-law even falsely testified she had forced them to read the Bible and go to church.

In the end, the Muslim siblings quarreled so much they were unable to go forward with the lawsuit.

So Inessa shifted tactics. She spread rumors her mother was mentally unstable and needed to be institutionalized. She even beat Mussalam, bruising her face and body. Notified of the assaults, police weren't enthusiastic about getting involved. But Anton was especially concerned when one of his siblings sent him a video clip of Inessa beating Mussalam in the courtyard of her own home.

And when Anton tried calling Mussalam and received no answer, he drove to his parents' town from his home in Russia to check out the situation.

Arriving at his parents' home, Anton pounded on the metal gate until his brother opened the small grille in the gate to see who was there.

"Anton is here!" he hollered toward the house. "What should I do?"

Hearing his brother mutter something from the house, he turned back toward Anton. "Goodbye. Go away."

"But where is Mother?" Anton insisted.

"She is in Tashkent with our sister," he replied. "She is ill." He closed the grille and walked away.

Anton felt uneasy. *Something is very wrong. Why wouldn't my brother let me in the house? I need to find Mother.*

The next morning Anton went to the police. One officer inadvertently revealed Inessa's plan to have their mother committed to a psychiatric hospital.

Anton couldn't believe his siblings would go that far but got in his vehicle and drove to the hospital. He was devastated and angry when he found his mother's name on the patient list.

Next, he drove to the school where his mother taught. That is where he learned she had been taken directly to the facility from her classroom.

"It was basically a kidnapping," Anton said. Inessa had bribed police to look the other way while she had her mother committed. Once in the hospital, Mussalam was administered drugs that fogged her thinking and made it impossible for her to even walk.

Meanwhile, Inessa's Muslim brothers locked down their father at home, not allowing him to have contact with anyone.

Anton insisted the chief of police have the hospital release his mother; soon Anton was allowed to take her home.

After enduring several weeks of drug "therapy," Mussalam wasn't the same woman she had been before. She struggled physically and mentally, and her memory was spotty—though she could recall vividly how she had been treated while a patient.

"The doctors would hold me down and give me shots," she said. And when Mussalam asked for help, the doctors and nurses told her, "You should have remained in Islam."

It took three years for Mussalam to fully recover from her time in the hospital. She's now able to work again and teaches part time. She'd take on more classes if she could; Uzbek law limits the hours a person of her age can work.

And she's recovered her ability to speak her mind, too.

During a court case that arose from her forced stay in the psychiatric hospital, a Muslim judge attempted to provoke her by asking why she had never made the Islamic pilgrimage to Mecca.

"Because it is a man-made institution that is not authorized by God," she answered boldly in open court.

Anton and his Christian sister now frequently visit and care for their parents, who faithfully attend one of the few churches in Uzbekistan that has received official registration since 2017.

And Mussalam's Muslim neighbors have welcomed her back to her home. Living with a loving Christian couple nearby has proven infinitely preferable to dealing with their quarreling Muslim children.

Mussalam could have ended the persecution she experienced at any time. All she had to do was deny Christ.

The beatings would have stopped, the character assassinations ceased. She would have been spared the nightmare of her time in the hospital.

But Mussalam continued following Christ despite opposition from her Muslim children. She persevered then—and she is persevering now, exemplifying the words of the apostle Paul to Timothy: "As for you, always be sober-minded, endure suffering, do the work of an evangelist, fulfill your ministry" (2 Timothy 4:5).

In the same way, whatever opposition you are experiencing for your faith and witness, endure it and look for ways to fulfill the ministry to which God has called you.

31

MAKING GOOD ON SECOND CHANCES

Hussein A.
Iran

He was a drug addict. A leader of a counterfeiting ring. A familiar face to prostitutes. And as Hussein looked down from atop one of Tehran's hundreds of high-rises, he considered how he had once thought such activities would bring him happiness.

They didn't. Now, in his twenties, Hussein had decided his life was beyond salvaging.

The distant Elburz Mountains, coated in a fresh blanket of snow, rose up boldly to eighteen thousand feet. In contrast, Hussein felt quite small, insignificant, and unnoticed—a meaningless speck among the nearly 10 million people in Iran's capital.

It is time, he thought, *to end my life.*

But his plan to do so was proving problematic. He was afraid to jump, so he decided to buy a little of the drug Ecstasy to take the edge off. Just as he exited the building and reached the streets, his cell phone rang.

"I've found something new," an old army buddy and fellow addict said. "Meet me for tea."

Perfect timing, figured Hussein. *A new drug to steel my nerves for the final plunge.*

"Tell me about the stuff you found," Hussein said to his friend soon afterward, cold hands wrapped around a mug of tea. "I'm interested."

"Not *stuff*," his friend corrected. "Not drugs. Much better. Jesus!"

Hussein nearly spit out his tea. He looked around to make sure nobody had heard. *"What?"*

"I've found Jesus," his friend told him in an excited whisper. "I've found peace. No more drugs. No more prostitutes. No more bullying people to make money."

Hussein was dumbfounded. But as his friend shared his story, something happened to Hussein: he stopped thinking about death. He stopped thinking about killing himself and started thinking about life.

Later, his friend had a Bible sent to Hussein, and then introduced him to a group of Christians who gathered in a local park.

"I'd thought of killing myself, too, before I found Christ," said one of the women who heard Hussein's story. "Do you want to give all the pain in your life to Jesus?"

He could think of no reason why he wouldn't. *A God who wants a personal relationship with me? A God who speaks of loving others? A God who forgives sins—who will love me even if I make a mistake or miss a prayer?* So Hussein received Jesus as his Savior and Lord.

"I still didn't understand what was happening to me," he recalled, "but I felt something was different. I knew my life was going to change. Christ just said he wanted me to be his son! This made me excited. This was very different from Islam. Immediately, I felt light, and I was unnecessarily happy for no reason."

He reveled in his newfound faith. Then came the testing, first by water and then by the authorities.

Hussein was at the beach, along the Caspian Sea, on a church retreat. He had never learned to swim, but egged on by his new friends, he splashed in the waves in chest-deep water. Suddenly, he took a step and couldn't touch the bottom. Panicked, he floundered, trying vainly to stay afloat. Then he began praying.

"Christ, give me one more chance." Months earlier, Hussein had sensed God calling him to ministry, but he had a good job, a house, and freedom, so he refused. Now he desperately longed to live, to have the opportunity to give up all he had for Jesus. "One more chance! I never ministered for you. I will minister for you if you do this. Just give me one more chance."

Several lifeguards dragged him to safety. Time would reveal whether his commitment had been born of true conviction or based only on a desperate will to live.

"You almost died," a church leader told Hussein after learning of his decision to surrender his life to Jesus. "You're feeling emotional right now. Do you know how hard it is to minister in Iran?"

"I don't care," Hussein said, sincere conviction in his voice. "I have to. Jesus gave me one more chance, and I have to do this. If I have to sacrifice everything I have, I will do this."

He quit his job, paid off his debts, and sold his car. Then he went into full-time ministry with a female coleader who ministered to women. As an evangelist, Hussein had a winning combination: his story was compelling, his passion convincing, and his message convicting. "The favor of the Lord was with me," he said. "I felt God had anointed me to witness." Dozens of people came to profess faith in Christ through his ministry—but he would pay a price for these souls.

In the Kurdish area of Iran, Hussein became involved with a group that distributed Bibles throughout the country. One day, just after five hundred New Testaments arrived, eight members of the Iranian secret police rushed into Hussein's home. They did not show any search warrants; they just ravaged his apartment looking for Christian literature.

The police handcuffed Hussein, along with three female church leaders, and whisked them away in a van. Blindfolded and shackled, Hussein and the others were transferred to another car. "This is just the beginning," one captor said smugly. "This is just the 'welcome parade.'"

Hussein prayed—not for himself, but that the small house church would not be destroyed. That the Bibles would not be confiscated. That their ministry would still find ways to keep proclaiming Jesus.

Hussein was placed in solitary confinement at the prison, in a room the size of a large bathroom. There was no bed, toilet, or sink; just two floodlights, one of which was kept on twenty-four hours a day to mess with his mind.

Are the women safe? he worried. *Did they reveal names of church leaders who will now be in danger? How can I warn them? Have the police discovered the Bibles?*

"Let's pray together."

Those words came out of nowhere—amid dead silence in a room where he was the only person, and he was not talking.

Hussein believes they were the words of Jesus: "I felt like Jesus put everything aside—the whole world aside—to come whisper in my ear. He said to me, 'There is no need for you to say anything because I am going to tell you what to say. Why are you afraid? At the end you are going to die, right? So why don't you just serve? Don't you have faith that when you close your eyes in this world, you will open them up to me? And when you open your eyes, you will be in my arms?'"

Hussein's interrogations began the next day. Whenever the evangelist's answers were deemed unsatisfactory, the interrogators kicked him in the stomach. After three days, Hussein was taken to court to face an apostasy charge, which in Iran can carry the death penalty.

"Why do you have a problem with mosques and imams?" a judge asked. "Why do you want to destroy Islam?"

Hussein was taken back to the main prison. He actually missed solitary confinement where he could pray to God without all the distractions.

"Only God can help you in here," a guard told him.

"Yes," said Hussein, "he *is* helping me."

Hussein was assigned to death row, where 250 inmates obeyed gang leaders instead of guards. Hussein prayed harder. That night, the gang leaders told Hussein to meet them at midnight in the bathroom. Instead of hurting him, however, they asked for his help. Did he have information about his prison friends in America?

Is there some mistake? Do they think I am someone else? Hussein had no prison friends in America, but the gang leaders believed otherwise and gave him first-class treatment. He got the top bunk and a private shower. He was given fresh vegetables.

After two days, when the guards offered to transfer him to a "safer" part of the prison, Hussein stunned them when he declined.

Eight days later, his family brought the deed to his house as collateral, and he was released on bail. During Hussein's hearing, the judge pointed out some mistakes in his appeal document and personally corrected them. "Here," he said, slipping Hussein a piece of paper. "This is my cell phone number. I'll personally supervise your case. And to make it more convenient for you, I won't require you to make the four-hour trip to the courthouse."

Again, Hussein was amazed by how God had intervened.

Police never discovered the five hundred Bibles that Hussein prayed would be kept safe—even though they sat in boxes in the middle of his living room.

He could only shake his head and praise God. "It was like when Paul was in jail and an earthquake opened the doors," he said. "Look how many doors God opened for me! This is why I want to keep serving, because I know God is with me."

How does Hussein see his future? The light of God has penetrated his darkest moments when he thought his life was over. With a grateful heart, he determined to continue serving God with the "one chance" he asked Jesus to give him. "They will either kill me, or there will be other miraculous events like these," he said. "Which one is bad?"

Hussein's words reflect what Paul wrote while in prison: "For to me to live is Christ, and to die is gain. If I am to live in the flesh, that means fruitful labor for me. Yet which I shall choose I cannot tell. I am hard pressed between the two. My desire is to depart and be with Christ, for that is far better. But to remain in the flesh is more necessary on your account" (Philippians 1:21–24).

While Paul was not afraid of death, as that meant being with Christ, he knew living meant meaningful ministry.

Through Christ, God has given us an amazing privilege of participating with him in "fruitful labor," as Paul wrote. How is the Lord calling you to be a part of his fruitful labor in your local church, in your neighborhood, in your workplace, in your community, in the world? Stop right now and ask him where your next step of obedient service should be.

32

WAKING UP

Bassam
Arabian Peninsula

Bassam sat in the long hallway outside the police commander's office, waiting for what promised to be a hard conversation. Christians being called in to defend themselves wasn't unusual in Bassam's community; he'd seen it happen often.

What *was* unusual was how Bassam was dressed.

He was wearing his police uniform.

Most people in his country cared more about keeping up appearances than embracing a deep faith in Islam, but having an openly Christian police officer was going to be a problem for authorities.

Bassam's decision to leave Islam and place his trust in Jesus Christ had happened eight years earlier, but he had kept quiet about it, meeting privately with the evangelist who had led him to his new faith. He worshiped at a small Christian fellowship when possible. But share his faith with others?

No way.

Then one day, Bassam came to a fellow Christian with an announcement. "I've been spiritually sleeping all these years," he told his friend and mentor, "and I can no longer keep my faith in Christ to myself. I feel strongly compelled to tell everyone about the only true God, Jesus."

And that's when Bassam's suffering began.

His wife immediately spurned him, telling her family she was married to an unclean man. And she made sure Bassam's fellow officers knew they worked with an infidel.

Bassam's commander initially took a conciliatory approach at their meeting. "We hear you have been deceived about a false religion," he said. "You should come back to Islam."

"No, Jesus is the true God," Bassam said, respectfully, "and I will follow him."

Frustrated, the commander told Bassam he could believe whatever he wanted, but he needed to keep his mouth shut about it. There would be no sharing his faith at work.

Bassam's wife wasn't satisfied with that solution. She and her family pressured the police department to discipline Bassam for professing his faith, something his supervisors were all too happy to do.

Soon Bassam was scheduled for multiple shifts in a row and summoned to meetings where he was bullied and threatened.

And there was no peace at home, either. When Bassam shared his faith with family members, his wife kicked him out of their apartment and limited his access to their daughters. His wife was careful not to divorce him. Doing so would cut her off from his salary and government benefits.

Bassam's brothers-in-law often beat him, sending him to the hospital numerous times with broken ribs, a permanently damaged knee, bruises, and bleeding.

Yet Bassam persisted in telling others about Jesus, even when his wife filed complaints in court accusing him of blasphemy against Islam, Muhammad, and the Quran. When called before judges, Bassam would simply tell them the truth: he believed in Jesus.

"That is okay," they replied. "Muslims believe Jesus is a prophet, too."

"No," Bassam responded. "I believe in the Jesus who is God who became human."

Bassam's declaration has cost him nights in jail for "apostasy."

Over time, Bassam has learned to be truthful but wise when testifying in court, trusting the Holy Spirit's inspiration.

Bassam's active faith is dangerous. His relatives could kill him as an apostate and receive a maximum penalty of only two years in prison—if they went to prison at all.

But Bassam refuses to stay silent. He continued sharing Christ with his father even after his father disowned him. And when his father was hospitalized, Bassam explained the gospel to his male relatives who came to visit. It was after he had received yet another beating for his boldness that one of Bassam's sisters sent him a message requesting a Bible. Since then, she and one of their brothers have secretly come to faith. One of Bassam's daughters has placed her faith in Christ, too.

One day, while Bassam was collecting tin cans along a roadside for extra income, a car suddenly braked beside him. One of his wife's brothers jumped out and beat him, breaking a tooth and bloodying his head before bystanders could intervene. His brother-in-law was arrested, but Bassam refused to press charges. "I love you," Bassam told him. "My Lord tells me to forgive."

That response prompted yet another sister to ask about Christ.

Bassam persists in speaking about Jesus and distributing Bibles to people on the street—knowing each day could be his last on earth.

An active faith that persists in proclaiming Christ comes at a cost.

Giving himself fully to Christ put Bassam on a collision course with his supervisors, his family, and his friends. They didn't understand his insistence on risking everything to faithfully fulfill his calling.

If that seems familiar, there's a reason. Jesus also didn't allow conflict or beatings to deter him. He stayed the course, a course that led him to the cross, an empty tomb, and a return to heaven.

A persistent witness can be costly, but we should give thanks to the Lord for the witness of Bassam and others like him as the apostle Paul wrote to the church in Thessalonica: "We ought always to give thanks to God for you... Therefore we ourselves boast about you in the churches of God for your steadfastness and faith in all your persecutions and in the afflictions that you are enduring" (2 Thessalonians 1:3–4).

33

ROLLING ON AMID THE RESISTANCE

Walid
Iraq and Lebanon

Walid rolls his wheelchair to his car and, with help from a companion, slips into the driver's seat. Yes, it would be easier to stay at home. It would be easier to just sit and watch television. It would be easier not to take a single risk. It was risk, after all, that had cost him the use of his legs.

"But," Walid asks, "how would God be served by that?"

Lives need to be saved for eternity. He has Bibles to pass out. He needs to make new connections with nonbelievers. So he turns the key and, thanks to hands-only controls, carries on with his ministry in the Middle East.

"We all have our crosses to bear," he explains. "I'm happy to bear this cross for the Lord."

Walid grew up in Mosul, Iraq. After becoming a Christian as a young adult, he moved to Lebanon to serve a church there.

Ironically, church leaders believed it best for him to return to Mosul and plant churches. For a missionary, being sent to Mosul was like a soldier being sent to the frontlines. But Walid welcomed the challenge.

The desert environment of northern Iraq is considered to be the Cradle of Civilization. Historic figures of the Old Testament—Abraham, Daniel, Esther, and Jonah—spent time there. Christians have lived there for more than two thousand years. But since 2003, more than a million Christians have fled Iraq.

The mass exodus and the dangers that caused it didn't deter Walid. He found an apartment in Mosul, connected with a community of believers, and began sharing the gospel with Muslims.

Walid made progress one conversation at a time. He shared the Word quietly, almost like a spy who has information to pass on but must do so undetected.

The chaos in Iraq has made Muslims increasingly open to Christ. Hundreds of thousands of Iraqis have died. Confronted with the possibility of death, they long for peace, joy, and assurance—hope they aren't finding in Islam. Many are seeking answers about the God of the Bible.

Walid's house church grew quickly. A handful of people became a dozen, then two dozen. Within five months, his congregation increased to sixty. In a place like Mosul, the tragic and sometimes deadly irony is that the more "successful" a church is, the greater the chance its members will be persecuted. Walid was certainly aware of what could happen, but he was not dissuaded.

"What is it, Walid?" his mother asked while riding in the passenger seat next to him. "You saw something in the mirror, no? Are we being followed?"

Walid glanced in his rearview mirror again and then toward his mother. "We're fine," he assured her.

"You cannot fool a mother," she replied. "Perhaps he thinks we are someone else."

The car behind them accelerated suddenly. Walid stepped on the gas too, but the pursuing car was too fast. Within seconds, it pulled alongside. Oncoming traffic swerved out of the way, kicking up dirt and rocks.

Walid was locked in panic, trying to protect his mother, avoid the other car, and not run into oncoming cars.

Pffft! Pffft! Pffft!

He felt the sting of a bullet in his back but managed to ease the car to the side of the road. As the assailant's car sped away, Walid felt as if he were going to black out.

"Mother, are you okay?" he managed to ask. "Were you hit?" He heard no answer.

Days later, at the hospital, his blurred vision sharpened. He could see his mother's face. She sat at his bedside, and a doctor explained what had happened.

"One bullet went through both of you," he said. "Walid, I am sorry. It hit your spinal cord. You will likely never walk again."

It was difficult news to hear.

"But your mother," said the doctor, "was lucky. She was struck only in the arm."

When visitors came, Walid never talked about himself. He spoke about how happy he was that his mother was not injured more severely. He shared how burdened he was for other evangelists in Iraq.

"They are carrying a bigger and heavier cross than most Christians," he said. "And despite the difficult situation, the salvation of souls is taking place in big numbers in Iraq. Pray that the Lord will intervene directly to strengthen, encourage, and empower us to do his work so that we can bring truth to Iraq."

Then he gripped the wheels of his chair, as if nothing had happened, and began rolling forward for God's glory.

Walid is a great example for us of 1 Thessalonians 3:7–8: "For this reason, brothers, in all our distress and affliction we have been comforted about you through your faith. For now we live, if you are standing fast in the Lord."

Regardless of the obstacles in his way, Walid perseveres. He knows he serves a God who will sustain his children through every kind of challenge. Walid reminds us that standing fast has absolutely nothing to do with our physical capabilities and everything to do with our resolve to hold firmly to God's promises, regardless of our circumstances.

What circumstances or physical limitation are you clinging to, claiming they are holding you back from being Christ's witness? Write them down and give them to the Lord. Declare God's goodness and commit to live out your faith daily as you stand fast in the Lord.

34

IN THE SHADOWS
NO MORE

Ibrahim
Yemen

Ibrahim wrapped his New Testament and carefully hid it in his backyard, shifting hand tools to make sure it couldn't be seen.

Once again, he hadn't been caught reading…but when would he finally be discovered?

Ibrahim had received the Bible from a customer visiting his small store five years earlier. The man asked Ibrahim—a devout Muslim—if he'd read the Bible.

"Of course not," Ibrahim said, stiffening. "It is full of errors and distortions."

But the man handed Ibrahim the book anyway. "Read it and find out for yourself."

Ibrahim agreed, but he still determined to make a note of every problematic verse he found in it.

For nearly a year, Ibrahim studied the New Testament, meeting with the customer who urged him to continue studying the Scriptures and to ask God to reveal the true way to him.

A deep peace flooded through Ibrahim followed by a stab of fear.

In Yemen, Christian converts from Islam can be sentenced to death. Muslims find it shameful when family members become Christians, and extremist groups like al-Qaida respond harshly.

For four years Ibrahim hid his Bible, sneaking into the backyard to read and pray. He was a Christian, but one hiding in the shadows.

Then, one day, it dawned on him: his fear made no sense.

If I believe in Jesus and he's given me eternity, why should I fear? he thought. *If they come to kill me, I will be ready to say, "Welcome."*

Ibrahim's fear vanished and was replaced with boldness. There were people he needed to tell about his faith—starting with his wife, Fatima.

Fatima was furious. Her husband had left Islam. He was a *kafir*—an infidel. Her home and family were ruined; her community was sure to turn on them when word got out. But for Fatima, it was more about betraying her family roots than just leaving Islam. Her grandfather had kept a handwritten genealogical record that traced the family back to Banu Hashim, the clan of the Prophet Muhammad. She wanted a divorce, but Ibrahim refused because it contradicted his Christian beliefs.

So Ibrahim and Fatima settled into a truce: they divided their home into separate living quarters, and Ibrahim agreed not to pray before their shared meals. On one occasion, their youngest son had innocently repeated his father's prayers while visiting Fatima's parents, nearly giving Fatima a panic attack. But both sides of the couple's families discovered the truth anyway—and both families disowned the couple. Ibrahim's parents even told neighbors their son had died in an accident, too ashamed to admit having an infidel son.

Ibrahim felt called to start a church, and several Christians suggested he plant one in a nearby city where many Muslims were coming to Christ. Ibrahim made frequent trips there to disciple Christian converts from Islam. All was going smoothly until Islamic extremists posted Ibrahim's name and personal information—including the address of his store—on the internet. They called Ibrahim the "leader of the Yemeni church," essentially painting a target on his back. They also claimed that he had forced people to stomp on the Quran, which Ibrahim had never done.

Now it wasn't a matter of whether he would be attacked, he realized. It was a matter of when—and where.

Ibrahim decided to leave Yemen, which also meant leaving behind his wife and two sons, his store, and the church he had planted. Other Yemeni Christians stepped in to lead the church. Fatima had conflicting feelings about Ibrahim's move. *I got rid of the problem*, she still thought.

Resettled in a neighboring country, Ibrahim focused on two things: finding a job and praying Fatima and their sons would come to know Jesus Christ. He landed a job working for a Muslim shopkeeper and shared the gospel with Yemeni immigrants he met in the marketplace.

Soon he led three expats like himself to Christ, and they formed a house church. Now there were four believers praying for Ibrahim's family.

Back in Yemen, Fatima was taking English lessons from an American woman who suggested she read the Bible so she would know more about her husband's religion. As Fatima read, she couldn't help but compare the Quran and the Bible. She found herself drawn toward Jesus Christ and his teachings about love, forgiveness, and mercy.

Fatima considered becoming a Christian but feared her family would kill her. *I feel like I am breaking from and betraying my family*, she thought, terrified.

Then one night, almost a year after Ibrahim left Yemen, Fatima dreamed about a man in white who told her not to be afraid. She awoke trembling and knew the dream must have come from God. So she fell to her knees and placed her trust in Christ as her Savior.

When she called Ibrahim to tell him the news, she heard shouts of "hallelujah!" blasting through her phone. Her husband's persistent prayers had been answered.

Two months later, Fatima and the boys joined Ibrahim.

But being Christians in their new home wasn't much easier than in Yemen. Ibrahim and Fatima struggled to raise their sons as Christians in a country where Islam is the state religion. Their teenage son, Yousef, was especially pressured to turn to Islam, but he held firm. He, too, had become a Christian.

On Yousef's seventeenth birthday, he answered a phone call from an unknown number. "Today is your birthday," the voice on the other end told him. "We don't want you celebrating with unbelievers."

A joke, thought Yousef, assuming one of his friends was playing a prank. So Yousef laughed it off, said goodbye to his mother, and headed to school.

Around noon, Fatima received a voice message from Yousef's cell phone. "We killed your son, and we will kill you too," a man said.

Ibrahim and Fatima raced to the school only to find Yousef wasn't there. Frantic, they rushed to the police who had nothing to offer.

Ibrahim's prayers were desperate and constant. "I trust you," he told God, "but this is really hard for me to bear." Even as Ibrahim encouraged his wife to be calm, his own heart felt as if it would explode out of his chest.

For Fatima, the passing hours were torture, and intense doubts filled her mind. "At least give me my son's body back so we can bury him," she silently pleaded.

Is Allah punishing me for leaving Islam? she wondered. Sobbing, she fell to her knees to ask God for help. As she prayed, she felt a wave of peace wash over her. Whatever happened, she knew she wasn't facing this horror alone. She sensed God was in control of the situation.

At 6:00 p.m. Fatima's phone rang. It was Yousef, calling from Yemen. Extremists had kidnapped him, her son explained. They'd flown him to Yemen, beaten him, and told him if he didn't embrace Islam his family would be killed.

Then the call abruptly ended.

Yousef held out for three days, terrified, before finally agreeing to do as his captors demanded. At that Yousef was released, on condition Yousef's friend—who'd been arrested for his part in the kidnapping plot—was also released.

Wary of further Islamist attacks, Ibrahim, Fatima, and their younger son, Omar, fled to Africa. Yousef joined them a few weeks later.

At first, Ibrahim's family struggled in their new country. They knew no one and didn't speak the language. They had no money and couldn't find jobs. And Yousef blamed his father for the suffering he had endured at the hands of the extremists. That bitter resentment tore at Ibrahim.

Cut off from believers who had encouraged them in the past, Ibrahim's family formed their own church, setting Thursday aside to eat together, read the Bible, and worship. They trusted God still had a purpose for them…but what?

Ibrahim applied for refugee status; throughout that process he was often with other Yemeni refugees. He told them his story, shared the gospel, and soon Ibrahim's family church became a house church ministering to Yemeni and Sudanese refugees.

Ultimately, Ibrahim turned one room in his house to a storage area for food items he collects and distributes to refugee families on a weekly basis. The ministry also pays school fees for several refugee children and distributes Bibles and memory cards loaded with digital Bibles. He has even outfitted a Yemeni youth soccer team with uniforms and equipment.

Not everyone appreciates his efforts, but still Ibrahim perseveres in serving others. He's heard the whispers: Is he giving help to lure Muslims away from Islam?

Ibrahim ignores the accusations. He perseveres.

Ibrahim's ministry has baptized more than a dozen Yemenis, and he expects to baptize more. The ministry team has planted churches that Ibrahim visits whenever possible, and he is reaching out to Yemeni refugees in other nations.

Yousef joined his father's ministry, serving Yemeni refugees and helping plant churches. Now in his twenties, Yousef earned a degree in biblical studies and is studying social media and video so he can better share the gospel and promote the church's events.

Ibrahim is grateful he's living in a time of harvest among Yemeni refugees. Since the outbreak of the civil war in Yemen, people have been more open to the gospel. They are hungry for hope—something Jesus Christ offers in abundance.

And Ibrahim is grateful God has enabled him to persevere in ministry. Whatever the danger, he's determined to stay the course.

He looks forward to the day he can return to Yemen.

Ibrahim's persistence wasn't just in searching Scripture or later looking for his son. He was persistent in prayer—and that's a good place for biblical disciples to be persistent.

Ibrahim's prayers—and ours—fuel our trust in God. Persistent prayer cements in our minds and hearts our reliance on God. And, as we see God's faithfulness in responding to us, we are reminded he's both loving and powerful.

Persist in prayer this week for Ibrahim and his ministry and others like him who are reaching Muslims for Christ at great risk. Like the apostle Paul, "keep alert with all perseverance, making supplication for all the saints, and also for me, that words may be given to me in opening my mouth boldly to proclaim the mystery of the gospel" (Ephesians 6:18–19).

Ask God to give them favor and strength as they speak boldly for Jesus Christ. Then ask the Lord whom he is calling you to persistently reach for Christ.

QUESTIONS FOR REFLECTION AND DISCUSSION

PERSEVERANCE

1. What image, story, or thought immediately comes to your mind when you think of the word persevere or perseverance? Why?

   a. *Merriam-Webster Dictionary* defines perseverance as "continued effort to do or achieve something despite difficulties, failure, or opposition."[1] Which of these words best describe what you have persevered against—difficulty, failure, or opposition? Explain.

   b. As you read the stories in this section about our persecuted Christian family members, what have they persevered against? What were they attempting to achieve? What story stands out? Why?

---

1. *Merriam-Webster.com Dictionary*, s.v. "perseverance," accessed March 16, 2023, merriam-webster.com/dictionary/perseverance.

2. Read Romans 5:1–5. For biblical disciples, endurance (perseverance) is not an end unto itself. As proclaimed in Romans 5, one does not endure suffering simply to declare victory. Perseverance tests us, steels us, and forms us into the people God wants us to be.

   a. What is the end result of the endurance of biblical disciples according to this passage?

   b. How can endurance produce character?

   c. How can character produce hope?

   d. What is the outcome of hope?

   e. Mussalam refused to allow the circumstances of her persecution make her bitter. Imagine your own family turning against you because of your commitment to Christ. Mussalam's testimony is one of a hope that can only be found in Christ as she endured suffering for the sake of the gospel. How does Mussalam's testimony inspire you to avoid letting bitterness weigh you down as you serve the Lord?

3. Persecuted Christians learn quickly that it is impossible to persevere in their own strength. As our intimacy with God grows, his strength empowers us to obey and endure faithfully regardless of the price we pay.

   a. Hussein of Iran, staring death in the face as he considered suicide, entered a transforming relationship with Jesus Christ because of the witness of a friend. Hussein's life was altered to the extent that he became an evangelist and house church leader. Though not every Christian has a conversion story as dramatic as Hussein's, every biblical disciple has an amazing story of transformation from spiritual death to eternal life.

b. What is your own story of transformation from spiritual death to eternal life by faith in Christ? Commit to sharing your story with at least one person this week.

4. Read Colossians 3:1–3.

a. What does the author of Colossians mean by "if you have been raised with Christ"?

b. What does it mean for biblical disciples to set their "minds on things that are above, not on things that are on earth"? Share some examples.

c. Why do we sometimes get so focused on earthly concerns that we neglect to pursue eternal thoughts and activities? How can having more of an eternal perspective give you a new lens through which to see every situation?

d. How can having an eternal perspective spur you toward perseverance?

Pray

Ask God for the ability to persevere through difficult circumstances, not as an end unto itself, but so you will become the biblical disciple God desires you to be—active in your faith. Pray for Christians, who experience persecution from Islamic extremists, to persevere so that God's redemptive purposes are realized in hostile areas and restricted nations.

Part V

FORGIVENESS

Bearing with one another and, if one has a complaint against another, forgiving each other; as the Lord has forgiven you, so you also must forgive.

Stories of Christians who are hated and violently persecuted because of their faith can be overwhelming when considering the suffering, pain, and grief they endure. What's more compelling are stories of how they forgive those who persecute them.

Forgiveness? Sincere forgiveness for the people who hate and harm them? Yes!

Among the stories in this section are a father who forgives a Muslim mob who drove him and his family from his home, a mother who forgives the men who killed her unborn child when they attacked her village, and a woman who forgives the terrorists who bombed her church and burned 85 percent of her body.

When such deep and sincere forgiveness is offered, it surprises us. It catches us off guard because forgiving those who persecute us is a distinctly supernatural act. Forgiveness for atrocities and murder committed against our loved ones is an abnormal human response—one we cannot accomplish in our own strength.

Yet Jesus commands his followers to do what is unimaginable. We are to bless people who abuse us. We are to love our enemies. And we are to forgive with the love and compassion Jesus expressed as he died on the cross, praying, "Father, forgive them, for they know not what they do" (Luke 23:34).

How is this possible? The path toward forgiveness is not easy, and forgiveness doesn't erase the painful consequences of wickedness. Are our persecuted brothers and sisters in Christ endowed with superhuman powers that make them eager to forgive those who perpetuate evil against them? No. Do they rationalize what has happened to them, so it is easier to deny and avoid their pain? No. Are they in some ways immune to the sinfulness of the human heart that drives us to anger, bitterness, revenge, and retaliation? No.

They struggle to forgive just as we do. The only difference is that they make the choice, in faith, to obey God. "Since God tells us in his Word to forgive," they say, "we must forgive."

Forgiveness is an obedient response to God, who graciously forgives and in Jesus has provided us an example to follow. There is no magic formula for generating a sincere desire to forgive. Nothing less than the power of a trusting relationship with God— knowing who he is—can nurture forgiveness in a wounded heart.

As our persecuted brothers and sisters in Christ say yes to God through obedience and by studying the Bible, praying, and seeking

to mature in their relationship with him, God accomplishes a
miracle in their hearts and minds. They see their abusers through
God's eyes. They learn to forgive! When deep trauma has occurred,
it may take a long time for that transformation to take place. But
God is patient, kind, and faithful to accomplish his good work in
the hearts of all those who seek, trust, and obey him.

35

WAITING FOR
THE BULLET

Abdu Oganesyan
Syria

Abdu awoke to the sound of screaming.

It was his own.

Abdu lay on the filthy concrete floor of a cramped cell, his elbows cinched behind his back and his hands and feet bound tightly. He struggled to breathe. His arms and legs felt as if they were on fire.

I'm dying, he thought. *And it can't come soon enough.*

As Syria's civil war tore his country apart, Abdu Oganesyan and his father decided to wait out the conflict in their small village. They sent Abdu's mother, sister, and younger brothers to safety in a large city outside of ISIS control, but Abdu and his father were determined to keep their workshop open. They also wanted to protect land that had been in their family for nearly a hundred years.

When clashes between the warring factions of the Free Syrian Army, al-Nusra Front, Islamic Front, and self-proclaimed Islamic State (ISIS) would erupt in their neighborhood, Abdu and his father hunkered down and tried to avoid getting caught in the crossfire. They fully expected to keep the shop open until the fighting was over.

But one day, their plans were thwarted.

Members of the Islamic Front—fighters from Iraq and Turkey—surrounded Abdu and a Muslim employee on the street in front of the shop.

The Islamists allowed the Muslim employee to leave, but slid a black bag over Abdu's head, put a gun to his temple, and shoved him into their vehicle.

A short drive later, the rebels bound his hands and legs, and threw him into a cell. They then sedated Abdu until he passed out.

When he came to, he was gasping in pain and in the presence of his kidnappers.

"What tribe are you from?" the leader asked.

But before Abdu could utter a response, another militia member answered for him. "He's not from any tribe," he sneered. "He's *Nasara*—a Christian."

The enraged leader spat angrily. "You should have killed him immediately!"

In a quest to rid their country of anything but Islam, Islamists like the Islamic Front and ISIS have targeted anyone who identifies with a religion other than their own. How active or uncommitted a non-Muslim may be doesn't matter.

The kidnappers spent days torturing Abdu. They cursed him and his parents, beat his feet with a stick, and forced him to stand facing a wall as they kicked him repeatedly while calling him a "Nasara pig."

They threatened to slaughter Abdu, questioning him as they ran razor-sharp knives across his legs, hands, and neck. "Who else in your village is a Christian? Which of those families have money?"

When he'd been beaten beyond questioning, Abdu was shackled with chains and dragged back into his cell—one his tormentors filled with scorpions and mice.

On the sixth day of Abdu's captivity, the insurgents forced him to call his family while they beat him to make him scream. They demanded the equivalent of $270,000 USD from his family—who had no way of paying the ransom.

Abdu's family was part of a traditional Christian church, but they'd never attended services. Only after moving to the larger city had his sister visited a church where she heard the gospel and placed her trust in Christ.

When the Islamists called demanding ransom, she recited part of Psalm 23 and told Abdu to remain hopeful because she and the church would pray for him.

Though Abdu had not yet made a decision to place his trust in Christ, he found himself repeatedly praying. "Lord, take me out of here, and I will become your servant."

On Abdu's tenth day in captivity, a guard gave him the news.

"It is over," the man told Abdu. "They will execute you."

One of the Islamists yanked off Abdu's blindfold, and for the first time he saw his captors' faces. Their heads and necks were wrapped in scarves. Showing Abdu no mercy, they loaded him into a truck and slammed the doors. When they arrived at a nearby creek, they again blindfolded him and ordered him out of the truck. "Kneel!" the agitators yelled at him.

Abdu's knees sank into the sand as his kidnappers gathered behind him.

"Please," he pleaded silently to the Lord. "Please let them kill me with bullets and not knives."

"Count to fifty!" ordered his captors.

He gasped as he waited for the blade or bullet that would end his suffering. He began counting to rein in his panic.

"One...two...three...four..." he said aloud, expecting to hear the sound of gunfire at any second.

But when he reached ten, he was surprised to hear the truck's engine grind to life.

"Eleven...twelve...thirteen...," he continued.

Abdu kept counting as he heard the truck speed away and, at fifty, cautiously lifted his blindfold.

His captors were gone.

Abdu was broken and bleeding, but he was free! Soon, he returned to be with his father.

Within a month, ISIS at last wrested control of the region from other Islamist groups and began erasing every trace of Christianity—and Christians. Sympathetic Muslim neighbors urged

Abdu and his father to leave while there was still time. "As soon as Ramadan[1] is over," they told them, "there will be killing."

So the two men abandoned their shop and walked away from their family land. They undertook a nerve-racking, eight-hour journey through the desert.

When they arrived at an ISIS checkpoint, Abdu handed over his ID knowing that his Christian name would surely be the death of him. But the guards simply sent him and his father on their way, no questions asked.

And when they finally approached a Syrian government checkpoint, soldiers were stunned to see two Christians emerging from ISIS territory. But they, too, sent Abdu and his father along into the relative safety of an area outside ISIS control in Syria.

After Abdu and his father reunited with the rest of their family, they packed up and moved to a neighboring country where Abdu decided to place his trust in Christ.

For Abdu, that faith has come to include forgiveness.

As he read the Bible, Abdu couldn't help but feel compelled by Christ's love to extend love to those who tortured him. "God can judge them," he determined. "I will love them."

---

1. Ramadan is the ninth moth of the Islamic calendar, which is based on the lunar cycle and is celebrated by Muslims around the world. The primary activity during Ramadan is fasting. From dawn until dusk, Muslims refrain from food, drink, and other pleasures, believing such abstinence shows their submission to Allah and serves as penance for their sins. At sunset, Muslims break the fast with a meal called *iftar*. Ramadan lasts for thirty days. Muslims believe that it was during Ramadan that the Quran was first revealed to their prophet Muhammad.

Abdu and his family cannot return to their home. Though ISIS was driven out of the area, they had built a mosque on Abdu's land. Local Muslims would never allow the mosque to be destroyed.

So, Abdu has started over. His earthly possessions are gone, but he's gained something more precious that can never be taken away: eternal life and a heart that experiences Christ's freedom to forgive.

How? How can Abdu forgive men who stole from him, spat on him, and tortured him?

He can't—at least, not on his own. That journey to forgive started as he studied God's Word. "Reading the Bible," he said, "reading all about God's love, and I thought, Maybe God loves us all." Abdu clings to Christ, letting the forgiveness he's received from Christ bubble up out of his life to others.

Forgiveness always carries the fingerprints of God. But that journey to forgiveness starts by spending time in Scripture and being caught up in Christ's love for us as reflected in 1 John 4:19: "We love because he first loved us."

If you're struggling to forgive, spend time in God's Word and ask him for help. Then act on what you learn.

36

POINT-BLANK FORGIVENESS

Habila Adamu
Nigeria

During a hot and humid night in northern Nigeria, quiet blanketed the village where Habila Adamu and his family slept in their concrete-block house. At precisely 11:00 p.m., someone pounded on his door.

"Come out!" a man shouted. "And bring your family too!"

Habila threw on clothes and gathered his wife, Vivian, and their young son. When he opened the door, intruders clad in robes and masks greeted him. His fear deepened. One man brandished an AK-47.

"We are here to do the work of Allah," the leader said emphatically as he gripped his weapon.

Too stunned to speak, Habila knew his words weren't nearly as important as the prayer he silently uttered: *Father, your will be done.*

The man asked Habila his name, where he worked, and whether he was a police officer or member of the military. Then he asked what proved to be the most important question: "Are you a Christian or Muslim?"

Habila did not hesitate. "I am a Christian."

Vivian realized these men were members of Boko Haram, a jihadi group responsible for the deaths of about ten thousand Nigerian citizens in 2014 alone.

"We are offering you a better life," one man stated, "if you will only say the shahada." The man taunted, "Go ahead, say it: 'There is no god but Allah, and Muhammad is his messenger.' Say it. Join us. Become a Muslim and join Boko Haram."

Habila glanced at his wife and son. "I am a Christian—and will always remain a Christian—even to death."

One of the men turned to Vivian. "If your husband does not cooperate, you will watch him die."

Vivian began to cry.

"A second chance, Mr. Adamu. Say the shahada." Habila remained silent.

"Your husband," said the jihadi, "is stubborn. Why can't you convince him to deny Christ and live a good life?" He raised the barrel of the rifle to Habila's head.

"Do not worry," Habila told his wife. "The death of a Christian is a great gain, not a loss."

"Bring me all the money you have," the man instructed Vivian. "Now!"

She scoured the rooms of their small home, grabbing anything of value that might convince these men to leave. The intruder was not impressed. He lowered the barrel to Habila's mouth. "Since you refuse to become a Muslim," he said, "here is your reward."

Bang! The bullet passed through Habila's mouth. He fell to the floor and lay still, blood pouring out. Horrified, Vivian screamed. Their little boy burst into tears.

"Shut up, woman!" an attacker yelled. "If you try to get help, we will find you and kill you—and your child."

One man kicked Habila's leg to make sure he was dead.

When they were satisfied that they had appeased Allah, they chanted, "Allahu akbar," and left.

Vivian bent down to the man she loved.

"I…am…still…alive," Habila whispered, straining. "Please… get help."

Vivian raced to a neighbor's home and called the police. They did not come. Finally, Vivian and her neighbors transported Habila to a hospital at 6:00 a.m.

"It is only by God's grace that he survived," a doctor told them.

Medical personnel scheduled Habila to undergo a bone graft to repair his cheekbone. Before the doctors began the operation, however, they were stunned to see that his cheekbone had virtually healed! The graft was unnecessary.

Once Habila recovered and returned home, he eagerly began sharing his story. Nearly every time he tells it, listeners ask the obvious question: "And how do you feel about the men who did this to you?"

Instead of talking about them, Habila speaks of forgiveness. "We are all condemned criminals," he says. "Jesus died for us. He loves us. That's why we must show that love to the people who hate us."

And that is why Habila has prayed the same prayer every day since the night he was shot. Echoing the words of Jesus as he hung on the cross, Habila prays, "God, forgive them. God, forgive them."

He prays earnestly that the men who came that night would find the same peace in Christ that he has. "I love them," he says. "If I have the opportunity to see them, I will hug them and I will pray for them."

"But how can you do that—forgive the people who nearly killed you, who nearly robbed your family of a husband and a father?" he is sometimes asked.

"Because," he replies, "Christ is love. The God I am serving is love. And he commands us to love one another." And that command includes our enemies.

Let Habila's words sink in for a moment: "God, forgive them. God, forgive them."

A few verses after Jesus taught his disciples to love their enemies, he told them to "forgive, and you will be forgiven" (Luke 6:37). By this, Christ was also saying, "Don't forgive, and you also will not be forgiven."

How is the Lord speaking to you through Habila's story and the words of Christ about your own willingness to forgive others? What step of obedience do you need to take?

37

WE WILL LEAVE
YOU IN PEACE

Jamil
Central Asia

As he had done nearly every night for three years, Jamil bent over the sink and washed the blood off his face. It was, he believed, a small price to pay for being hated because he loved and proclaimed Jesus. But soon he reached a breaking point.

Jamil was raised in a moderate Muslim family in Central Asia, in an area south of Russia, north of Iran and Afghanistan. At one point, his brother had adopted such radical beliefs that he was put in prison. For Jamil, that event triggered deep soul-searching.

During his quest for spiritual truth, he met Christians who shared the gospel with him. Jesus, he realized, was all that Allah was not. The one true God. The promised one. The Savior.

Jamil accepted Christ with gusto. He began sharing his faith as if he were a dying man who found water in the desert and wanted to give it to everyone who was thirsty. And people he met were thirsty for the gospel. He led his brother, a former Islamic extremist, to Jesus Christ. Then he led three other siblings to Christ. He planted four house churches.

After getting married and then fathering a son, Jamil accepted an offer to be a missionary in another part of Central Asia. He moved his family to a village comprised entirely of Muslims. When word spread of this Christian, this kafir, the nightly beatings began.

Each time, Jamil refused to retaliate. Instead, he shared Scripture verses with his attackers. But one night the beatings went too far. A lone man had come to assault him. As Jamil endured the punches, his six-year-old son walked into the room. The attacker thrust his fist into the child's stomach. The boy crumpled to the floor, writhing in pain.

Instinctively, Jamil rushed to protect his son. Jamil's turn-the-other-cheek spirit gave way to an adrenaline-fueled lust for revenge. When the attacker fled, Jamil found a knife and raced into the night after him.

When Jamil burst into the home where the man lived, the man's elderly father was sitting in the front room.

"Where is your son?" demanded Jamil, breathless, his eyes like those of a madman. "I am going to *kill* him!"

"Jamil, this isn't like you," the elderly man replied. "Why do you want to kill my son?"

"I can take the beatings," he answered. "I cannot take the beating of my son, which is what your son just did."

Momentarily deterred by a father who, like him, loved his son and did not want to see him hurt, Jamil continued on through the village. Everywhere he went, he spewed threats of revenge to anyone who would listen—and to some who wouldn't.

"Anyone who touches my son," he promised, "I will *kill!*"

Jamil could not sleep when he returned home that night. It wasn't just the attack on his son that troubled him. It was the guilt he felt for sinking as low as his attacker and vowing to extract justice by using violence. He knew what he had to do.

Before the sun rose, he walked to the home of the man who had attacked his little boy. Although the son and his father feared retaliation, Jamil had not come for revenge.

"I am sorry for my threat," he said humbly. "I do not want to kill you. I do not want to kill anyone. Please forgive me."

Despite his appeal for forgiveness, the nightly beatings continued. One night the leaders of the local Islamist group were about to leave on a hunting trip. They barged into Jamil's home to beat him, and then turned to his wife.

"You," one man demanded, "cook for us."

The men took their places around the table as if daring her to refuse. Jamil's wife looked at her husband, uncertain how to respond.

"Please," he said, "cook for them."

So she prepared a meal for the men who sat at her table—the same men who routinely beat her husband. As the men waited, Jamil said, "It does not matter how cruel you have been to me or to anyone else. God will forgive you and accept you into his kingdom if you repent and place your faith in Christ." He paused. "May God bless your hunt."

The men looked at him, and then at each other, in disbelief. "We came here to eat your food and to beat you," stated the leader, "but now we cannot." He looked at the others and continued. "We will leave you in peace."

Days later, the leader invited Jamil to his home. "Please," he said, "share with my family what you shared with us the other night."

It was the first time one of his tormentors asked to learn about Christ—and it would not be the last.

God's message of love and forgiveness is available to all people, as affirmed in John 3:16: "For God so loved the world, that he gave his only Son, that whoever believes in him should not perish but have eternal life." The bold love of God can reach our enemies. It is powerful enough to melt even the hardest heart. His forgiveness transforms the coldest heart.

We cannot thwart the evil intentions of those around us in our own strength. But the Holy Spirit within us can disarm even the most vicious people as we faithfully demonstrate God's love and forgiveness. What finally allowed Jamil the opportunity to share God's love with these hateful men was forgiveness and bold love. It certainly isn't easy for a father to forgive someone who intentionally injures his child. It isn't easy for a woman to cook dinner for the men who beat her husband and son. And it isn't easy to bless those who hate us. But that is the path of forgiveness.

Let us pray diligently for our persecuted brothers and sisters who suffer in the battle against evil. Pray that those who fight against the faithful will see God's love and forgiveness in action and realize that he provides another way. Pray that they will be set free from their bondage to hatred and evil.

38

FINDING GRACE
IN THE SCARS

Fenny
Indonesia

Sunday, May 13, 2018
6:30 a.m.

Two young men, ages 16 and 18, rev their motorbike engine as they speed toward their target—Saint Mary Immaculate Catholic Church in Surabaya. A young mother, with her two sons and niece, walks through the church gate and notices the bikers and braces for the worst. Just a dozen feet past her, the teens detonate their satchel of explosives, knocking her to the courtyard cobblestones, rendering her temporarily blind and deaf.

As the world slowly drifts back into focus, she raises her head and sees a security guard's dead body. She stares at her bloody hands and is then slammed with panic.

The children! she thinks, *My God, where are my children?*

Amid the shouts, smoke, and chaos, she can hear one of her son's cries of agony—but can't see him. She staggers to her feet, stumbling toward his screams.

She finds him on the ground near her niece, who is also conscious. She calls for her other son, but gets no reply. Then she spots his lifeless, twisted body just a few feet away. She tries to pick up her sons, but her ankle buckles, sending her back to the blackened cobblestones. Shrapnel has sliced through a tendon and, though she can't yet feel them, she's gasping through a tangle of broken ribs.

She pleads for help as parishioners stampede past her. One man stops, calls over another security guard, and the two carry her sons to the man's car. As her boys are rushed to the hospital, the young mother collapses against the church gate, praying as the car speeds away.

Soon a fellow parishioner wraps an arm around her, helping her into his car so she can get to the hospital.

7:15 a.m.

Three miles west of Saint Mary, a woman and her two daughters, ages nine and twelve, step out of a black Toyota minivan that's stopped in front of Indonesia Christian Church. The females are wearing tan *niqabs*, veils worn by some Muslim women that reveal only their eyes.

The three walk slowly and calmly toward the Protestant church as the minivan glides back into traffic.

Sensing something wrong, a church security guard approaches the trio, intent on stopping them from entering the church building.

The woman, who carries a large bag over one shoulder, quickens her pace toward the church. Then, before the guard can tackle her, she detonates the bombs she's carrying, killing herself and her two daughters.

The explosion isn't powerful enough to kill anyone else. Even the security guard, just inches away, survives the blast.

A short time later, that same black minivan approaches another church, located two miles northwest.

It crawls up the center of the street, then turns sharply to the left, aiming directly at the church building.

7:53 a.m.

Fenny Suryawati is standing at the bottom of a staircase near Surabaya Central Pentecostal Church's main entrance when the black minivan rams the church's gate, striking two parking attendants.

Five bombs inside the vehicle erupt into an immense ball of fire, igniting gas tanks in five cars and thirty motorcycles parked nearby.

Flames sear the front of the church building and immediately envelop Fenny, who is on her way to pick up her daughter, Clarissa, from Sunday school.

"Help!" Fenny cries out as the heat of the fire becomes unbearable. Church members rush toward the inferno to pour water on her smoldering skin, bringing relief Fenny knows will not last.

As flames consume the church's entrance, Fenny's pastor is leading thirteen hundred worshipers when he hears an explosion. It must be an electrical fire, he thinks, but he can't see anything because of the black smoke rolling into the sanctuary. The pastor urgently directs congregants to exit through the back door.

When police inform the pastor that the church was attacked and people are injured, he quickly organizes transportation so the wounded won't need to wait for ambulances.

Fenny lay in an evacuation area where she is finally reunited with her husband, her mother-in-law, and Clarissa. When Fenny sees her daughter's injuries—burns on her forehead, stomach, and hands, and a shrapnel wound to her mouth—she breaks down in tears.

A church member helps Fenny and Clarissa into the back seat of his car and speeds toward the hospital. The driver is unsure if Fenny will survive long enough to receive care.

During the ride to the hospital, Fenny's senses catch up with her physical condition. She doesn't feel heat anymore, but she smells her own burning flesh. All she can think about is Clarissa. *Why was her body injured like that?* she wonders.

Two Minutes Later

Fenny's stretcher is rushed through the hospital's swinging doors into an already chaotic emergency room.

Doctors place her in a tub of warm water to stop the burning, and then stitch up the open wounds above her eyes and on her upper lip. She is taken into surgery to remove shrapnel embedded in parts of her body. One pierced her left side, just missing her lungs.

Though she doesn't know it yet, the trauma of the blast has twisted her body, and flames have melded her fingers together. Clothing melted into her flesh must be removed, debris scraped from her scorched flesh. She sustained burns over 85 percent of her body. Her face and head are swollen, and her hearing is gone.

• • •

The deaths at the three churches weren't the only ones caused by the Islamic radicals that day. At 9:00 p.m., three members of a Muslim family were killed when a bomb detonated prematurely in their apartment. The following morning, a bomb exploded at the Surabaya Police headquarters, wounding four officers and killing four suicide bombers out of a family of five. The surviving family member was an eight-year-old girl.

In all, twenty-eight people (including thirteen suicide bombers) died and fifty-seven more were injured in the attacks.

Among those killed were the two sons of the young woman from Saint Mary Immaculate Catholic Church. The young mom and her niece were among the injured, with the niece suffering a broken right wrist as well as severed nerves in three fingers on her right hand.

Authorities report the self-proclaimed Islamic State (ISIS) ordered the attacks as revenge for the imprisonment of a radical Islamist leader who was prosecuted for his role in previous attacks.

• • •

Fenny's recovery has been painful and slow. She's endured thirty skin grafts, surgery, and radiation treatments to kill the malignant cells that formed in her healing body.

And in addition to physical therapy, she has faced emotional and spiritual challenges as well.

She experienced depression because she could not do normal things, like wash herself, clean her house, or even hold a spoon. "Why did it happen?" she asked God. "When will the suffering be over?"

Through a government program to help the survivors overcome their trauma and to help former terrorists see the consequences of such violent acts, Fenny met with former radicals who have repented of their actions.

"I didn't want revenge because they said they had been indoctrinated, and they expressed sorrow for what they had done," she said of the meeting. "I never felt bitterness toward them. If I did, what good is that?"

Fenny has moved from asking, "Why me?" to asking, "Why am I still alive?"

The answer, she found, is in Christ.

When she senses people staring at her scars, she quietly asks God, *How can I be used in this situation?* When people ask about her burns, she eagerly tells them about Christ. She wants him to use her story and pain to advance his kingdom.

After years of hard, painful work, she is once again able to do practical, daily tasks. And she is determined to serve God, learn to ride a motorbike again, look for a job, and share her story.

"I was a believer before," she said, "but after the bombing, I felt I couldn't serve my family or God anymore.

"But I began to understand much more about the grace of God. Even when I couldn't do anything, it was still there. It was no longer me anymore, but him instead."

The scars cannot hide her bright smile. "I understand grace much more now."

Survivors of such brutal attacks still struggle physically, mentally, and spiritually. And it's that last struggle that puts forgiveness front and center.

Fenny will never again have the life she lived before the attack. Playing tag with her daughter, moving freely through her day—those are things of the past.

While she is reminded of her losses daily, Fenny holds her hurt with open hands, asking God to do his work in them. And she asks for his grace to flow through her to others reflecting the words of Hebrews 12:15: "See to it that no one fails to obtain the grace of God; that no 'root of bitterness' springs up and causes trouble, and by it many become defiled."

God will honor Fenny's faithful desire to embrace his grace in the journey to forgiveness...and he will honor yours.

Whom do you need to forgive?

And are you willing?

39

THE JOURNEY OF FORGIVENESS

Pauline Ayyad
Gaza City

In terms of dangerous professions, directing a bookstore wouldn't be on the list of high-risk occupations. Certainly, being a logger, deep-sea fisherman, or high-rise window washer would be dangerous. But a bookstore director? No. Unless it is a Christian bookstore in a place where some view the Christian faith as a threat.

Rami Ayyad ran such a bookstore for the Palestinian Bible Society in Gaza City, a Muslim-dominated urban center of half a million people in the Gaza Strip. The store served about thirty-five hundred Palestinian Christians who lived in Gaza City, most of whom belonged to the Greek Orthodox, Roman Catholic, or Baptist denominations. In Hamas territory, individuals sometimes pay a high price for identifying with such groups. That was what made Rami's work dangerous and it would cost him his life.

One evening in October 2007, three men showed up at the bookstore. "They are fundamentalists with long beards," Rami said in a phone call to his family before the men abducted him. Early the next morning, his body was found near the store—scarred with bullet holes and knife wounds.

• • •

Rami and Pauline had been active members of their church for years. Rami was working at a bank to provide for his family. God had put it in their hearts to serve him, but at that time, they did not know what kind of ministry God wanted them to do.

Two years before his death, Rami sensed God calling him to quit his banking job and lead a Bible Society ministry in Gaza called "The Teacher's Bookshop." Because the ministry was located in a church building that received frequent threats and had been bombed on two occasions, Rami's career change worried Pauline.

"I am not comfortable because I have a lot of fear," she told Rami, knowing he was at peace with the decision. The couple had two young children at the time.

Rami prayed about the position, then told his wife, "I need to obey what God placed on my heart."

Pauline's initial anxiety decreased after Rami started his new job at the bookstore, and the two of them began leading programs such as a children's Bible study. For Pauline, it became normal life, and the fear subsided.

On several occasions, however, Rami was threatened. One of those occurred a few weeks before his murder. A local sheikh entered the shop and told Rami he should convert to Islam.

"I cannot make you be a Christian," Rami replied, "and you cannot make me be a Muslim."

"I know how to make you become a Muslim," the sheikh threatened.

When Rami mentioned the confrontation to his wife just two days before he was abducted, his attitude reflected only peace and acceptance of the danger he faced. "What can they do?" he said confidently. "The only thing they can do is to kill me, and then I will be killed for Christ."

But Pauline struggled to understand how he could be so calm, so happy. He was speaking like he was ready to die for his faith, like God was preparing him—and Rami was ready.

Around the same time, several men Rami recognized followed him home one day and stared at him menacingly. But since local authorities had done little about previous threats to the bookstore, Rami and Pauline felt there was nothing more they could do to ensure their safety.

On Oct. 6, 2007, around 4:30 p.m., Rami closed the bookstore and headed home. Shortly afterward, he called his sister on a number she didn't recognize, and she overheard him saying, "What do you want from me? I don't know you!"

When Rami didn't arrive home at the expected time, Pauline began to worry and called the Bible Society's leaders. But they hadn't heard from him either. Then, about 6:00 p.m., Rami called Pauline. "I am on a long trip and will be gone for a while," he said.

The next morning, Rami's brother called to tell her that some-one had found Rami's body.

Pauline, who was four months pregnant with their third child, was devastated. As she prayed and wondered why this had hap-pened, she remembered Romans 8:28: "And we know that for those who love God all things work together for good." But she wasn't ready to accept the reassuring words of Scripture. *What good thing can come through killing my husband?*

Pauline's relationship with the Lord suffered for months after Rami's murder. She was angry with God. "Why did you allow Rami to be killed?" she asked. "Why did you allow us to marry in the first place?"

For the next five years, Pauline battled depression as she struggled with grief. "God, you made me a widow; why are my kids without a father?" she asked again and again. While those years were difficult, she knew Jesus Christ was still with her. She would wake up and look to him for strength. When she dwelled on her situation, she got depressed; but when she looked to God, he would lift her up.

While working through her grief, Pauline grew angrier toward the men who killed her husband. Living in a predominantly Muslim area, she heard the Islamic call to prayer five times a day—and each call from the minarets served as a potential provocation.

Pauline would get upset when Christian friends urged her to forgive Rami's killers. *It is easy for you to say to forgive when your lives have not been destroyed*, she thought.

Christians also encouraged her to pray that Rami's killers would come to know Christ so they could go to heaven. Pauline refused. *For them to receive Christ and go to heaven is not acceptable*, she thought.

Eventually, Pauline's anger escalated into rage, especially around the anniversary of Rami's murder. But in the end, the growing anger exhausted her. She started praying a specific prayer. "I know that I am your daughter, and I know that I need to forgive—but I can't forgive. Help me; let me be able to forgive in a way that is real." Pauline repeated that prayer regularly for a year.

Five years after Rami's death, Pauline and her children attended a conference about forgiveness. At one point, a pastor asked members of the audience to close their eyes and imagine a person they needed to forgive. Pauline immediately imagined the man who had killed her husband. She knew God wanted her to forgive him.

On the last day of the conference, the pastor asked if anyone wanted prayer to help them forgive someone.

Pauline responded.

"I want to forgive!" she cried out to God as other Christians gathered around her. In that moment, she felt the Holy Spirit touch her soul. When Pauline opened her eyes, she felt like a new person. She used to tell God, "You are mad at me because I won't forgive." And she would hear him say, "Yes, because you are my daughter, and you need to forgive."

After the conference, Pauline began to study what the Bible says about forgiveness. She realized that not to forgive is a sin. She used to believe that it was her right not to forgive.

But her forgiveness was going to be tested.

When authorities arrested the man thought to be Rami's killer, Pauline's anger was rekindled, and she immediately reacted. *I want him to die the worst death ever and go to hell!* She had worked so hard to overcome her feelings toward her husband's killer, but now she was struggling. *I think I might lose my forgiveness toward him.*

In addition to Rami's murder, the man was suspected of killing a Hamas leader and some Palestinian police. For Pauline, it was like Satan was giving her wicked thoughts about the person who had killed Rami…the person who made her a widow.

But God reminded Pauline about her testimony: that Rami had died because of his faith in Christ, and that she had already forgiven her husband's killer. Soon after repenting for her unforgiving thoughts, Pauline made her forgiveness public. She posted online that she had renewed her forgiveness toward the man and prayed for a blessing in his life.

Pauline's public display of grace angered many people, including some in her own family who wanted vengeance. After struggling to tell her children about the pressures she faced and that Hamas planned to execute the killer, she finally asked her oldest son, George, what he thought of the man who had murdered his father.

Pauline was shocked by his answer.

"I forgive him, and I pray that he will go to heaven and meet with my dad," George told her.

On the eve of the man's execution, Christians in Rami's family urged Pauline not to speak about forgiveness again. But just as her husband had insisted years before, she believed she needed to obey God.

On the day of the execution, Pauline posted another message. After describing the suffering she had endured since Rami's death, she explained that God had led her to forgive his killer. "Justice is in the hands of God," she emphasized.

Pauline was shocked when she learned how the Lord used her online post to change people's hearts. Individuals who were against her were now with her…including Rami's family. After they read her message, they told her they would forgive too.

For Pauline, the process of reaching total forgiveness didn't happen overnight. "Forgiveness is a decision," she said. "That is what I experienced.

"You cannot forgive by your own strength, but when you have this will, a real will, an honest will to forgive and you put it in front of God, God will help you to forgive. I thought I had forgiven already, but God prepared me until I could enjoy true forgiveness."

Losing a loved one always hurts; that pain is a testament to how much that person meant to us. But bitterness in the heart poisons a biblical disciple's ability to live a Christ-honoring life. When Pauline was able to truly forgive her husband's killers, she was set free from bitterness, which opened her life to new possibilities.

The catalyst for Pauline was not only saying she forgave Rami's killers but also being certain in her soul that she had forgiven them. Once she allowed God to wash away her bitterness, she was free to begin living an abundant life for his glory.

And like Pauline, sometimes that forgiveness is tested...deepened.

Besides bitterness, the consequences of unforgiveness are real. Christ said, "For if you forgive others their trespasses, your heavenly Father will also forgive you, but if you do not forgive others their trespasses, neither will your Father forgive your trespasses" (Matthew 6:14–15).

Christ's words are that clear, that simple, and that hard. If we want to experience forgiveness from our heavenly Father for our own sins, then we must forgive those who have wronged us.

Right now, ask the Lord if there is any unforgiveness in your heart toward people who have wronged you, and then ask him to help you forgive them in his strength. As Pauline cried out among her brothers and sisters in Christ, he longs to hear you cry out: "I want to forgive!"

40

FACE TO FACE WITH HER ASSAILANT

Amina
Nigeria

In the northern Nigerian village of Kataru, darkness mirrored the evil that lurked in the early morning quiet. As she lay in bed in her mud-walled house that April morning, Amina Yakubu was awakened by a slight tug in her abdomen. *Ah, just the baby kicking again.* Six months pregnant with her third child, Amina drifted back to sleep. Her husband was away hunting.

Ch-ch-ch-ch-ch-ch-ch-ch-ch-ch-ch-ch-ch-ch.

Amina bolted upright. *Machine-gun fire?* She called to her friend who was staying in the adjacent room. "Get the children! Fulani!"

A year earlier, a group of militant Islamic Fulani massacred more than five hundred men, women, and children in a nearby village. Amina never thought it would happen where she lived. But just in case, she had created a secret hiding place for the children.

She and her friend threw on some clothes and gathered the half-asleep youngsters. She quickly patted her abdomen. "It's okay, baby. It's—"

A noise outside the house ramped up her fear.

"Out the back," she whispered to her friend. "Over the fence. I'll go first. Hand me the children."

God, help us, she prayed silently as she tried to get her pregnant body over the fence. Partway up, her leg exploded in pain from a bullet. She dropped back to the ground, narrowly missing a child.

Her friend dragged Amina back to the house, leaving a bloody trail, with kids in tow. She locked the door and shuffled the children into the hiding place.

Seconds later, the door flew open. One of the Fulani militants raised a machete above his head. Amina raised a hand to block the blow, but he sliced the blade into her scalp, neck, and arms. She slumped to the floor, left for dead in a pool of blood. Not finding anyone else in the house, he left to help set fire to the village.

Hours later, Amina awoke in a hospital, transported there by a Nigerian army crew. Her baby was delivered stillborn. It took doctors a long time to suture all her wounds. It took even longer for her to stop sobbing.

With her husband by her side, Amina mourned the loss of her baby.

"Those who did this to you," her husband asked, "if the army brings them to you and you see them, what will you say should be done to them?"

Amina paused. Even speaking was difficult. "Do to them… what they…did to…me."

He looked away, then back into her eyes. "You won't forgive them?"

"I will…never…forgive them," she whispered.

Weeks passed in the hospital. Weeks to reflect. Weeks to pray. Weeks to consider God's will, not hers.

Then her husband asked the question again.

"If I see those who attacked me, if they are arrested and brought to me, I have forgiven them," she replied. "All this suffering I am going through, even before it happened, I know that the Lord had already known and he has written it, that at so-and-so time I will find myself in this suffering. Therefore, I will forgive them."

Four months later, Amina was discharged from the hospital. Four months after that, she was at her mother's house when a man came to deliver firewood. Their eyes met. It was the man who had attacked her. She knew it. He knew it.

Amina's heart almost split open as all the painful memories of that day came flooding back.

The man looked everywhere but at her. He put the wood down, received his pay from her mother, and left.

Her uncle later chastised her for not speaking up. He wasn't interested in Amina telling the man she had forgiven him. Her uncle wanted her to alert him so he could beat the coward to a bloody pulp.

"I don't have any bad intention against them," she said. "Our prayer is that they should understand what they are doing is not

good, so that they will be saved when they die or when our Lord
Jesus will come. Because if they died in this habit, they will not
see God."

*Forgiveness has not been easy for Amina, who trusts in God for justice.
She has clung to the words of the apostle Paul: "Beloved, never avenge
yourselves, but leave it to the wrath of God, for it is written, 'Vengeance
is mine, I will repay, says the Lord'" (Romans 12:19).*

*"I am pleading with God to give me a courageous heart, that he
will give me patience so that I will not betray his name," she said. "I
should hold on to God no matter the suffering or persecution. Every
day I ask him that in all of this suffering he will give me courage, that
nothing will tempt me to turn back from him."*

*Amina, like so many other persecuted Christians, reminds us that
we, too, can forgive people who have committed offenses toward us.
Her prayers for the salvation of those who do evil are prayers that
need to be on our lips. Her prayer for the courage to forgive so that we
do not betray God's name is a prayer that needs to be in our hearts.
But sometimes it is difficult to find the words to pray. The psalmist
declared, "Even before a word is on my tongue, behold, O Lord, you
know it all together" (Psalm 139:4).*

*Open your heart and your thoughts to the Lord, so that he can
lead you in the way everlasting—a way that leads you to forgive.*

41

FORGIVING YOUR ENEMIES IS GOOD

Diya
Somalia

A warm wind blew dust into the Somali sky, creating a brownish haze—just like most days. Fishing boats bobbed on the Indian Ocean beyond. Muslim women wrapped in colorful clothing walked briskly to market, their veils obscuring all but the roundness of their faces.

In a culture that believes some things must be covered up, Diya was a quiet rebel. He had trusted in Christ, as had his wife, Aniso, and their six-year-old son, Amiir. For nearly two decades, this Muslim-turned-Christian had gone against the grain of conventional thinking. He refused to hide his Somali-language Bible.

His decision was not motivated by pride. He loved this book for a number of reasons, and he felt no need to hide it away as if it were something shameful. It was also one of his few possessions that survived a 1991 house fire triggered by the civil-war outbreak. Even more important, it was God's Word.

Some of its scorched pages were still legible, and Diya read from them every day. His favorite story featured Abraham, who was going to sacrifice his son when an angel provided a ram to save Isaac's life. He also liked the promise in the New Testament that Jesus had become like that ram—a sacrifice for all of humanity's sin.

"When I read the Bible, I was reassured knowing that Christ is always with me," Diya reflected. That is exactly what he was doing when Amiir watched his father read the Bible and then set it aside.

Sharing his father's love for God's Word, Amiir took the Bible—with the big, bold cross engraved on its cover—and sat on the crumbling curb outside. He stretched out his feet in the dirt and opened up the book, just like his dad. As the morning bustle picked up, he watched passersby carefully in hopes of recognizing some of his little friends.

Suddenly, a vehicle pulled up near Amiir, kicking up a cloud of dust. Out rushed two soldiers, members of the Islamic Courts Union, a militant tribal alliance that controlled most of southern Somalia. Their motto: "There is no God but Allah; Muhammad is the messenger of God."

"Little boy," asked one, "where did you get that book you are holding?"

"It is Papa's," he replied proudly.

"And where is Papa?"

"Inside," Amiir said, nodding back at the house.

The soldiers knocked on the door. When Diya opened it, a soldier rammed the butt of his rifle into his head.

"Papa!" screamed Amiir.

Diya crumpled to the ground, unconscious. Amiir ran to him, wailing in grief. Aniso bent over her husband, one arm wrapped around her son in a comforting embrace.

"Why have you done this?" she asked the radicals, eyes ablaze in anger. She pulled her son to her chest.

Bang!

The bullet killed Amiir instantly, passing through his head and into his mother's stomach. She died later at a hospital.

Diya recovered and avoided arrest for having the Bible, but only because a tribal leader intervened on his behalf. Months later, he said the deaths of his wife and son made him stronger, and that he has forgiven the man who killed his family.

"Loving and forgiving your enemies is good," Diya said. "I know my wife and son are with Jesus Christ. Everything that has happened, has happened by the grace of God. And I am closer to Jesus than before. I don't have it as bad as some others. There are other people who have been through worse treatment than me. These things happen, and this is how we live."

Still, it is a struggle for him to care for his two remaining sons alone. He grieves for the playful little boy he lost because of his Christian faith. Yet Diya also longs to grow in his faith and love God as Abraham did when he was willing to give up everything for God—even his son.

Life in a place where persecution is as intense as it is in Somalia is extremely difficult. Diya and his fellow believers welcome the prayers and support of the global body of Christ to help shoulder the burden they carry. Jesus knows the heartache and challenges his followers face when they give up everything for him. It is those who are faithful in giving it all whom Jesus declares to be "worthy of me" (Matthew 10:37).

Father, I mourn with my persecuted Christian family today because of their loss. I ask for comfort for Diya and others who have lost loved ones because of their faithful witness. I join Diya in asking that those who killed his loved ones repent, turn to Christ, and work to advance Christ's eternal purposes. Amen.

42

FEAR IS A DISEASE

Dereje Tekle
Ethiopia

Dereje stands at the front of a mission school classroom. Eager faces look up as Dereje gathers his thoughts and walks around the podium to stand close to the students.

Dereje won't need notes for this talk. He hasn't come to share information; he's here to share his story.

"When I was a student in this school," he says, "there weren't many Christians living in my region. When we came close to Muslims, they'd cover their noses because they considered us stinky. They hated us. I began thinking that Muslims had a bad spirit.

"But while here I learned what Islam is and what Muslims lack," says Dereje. "God gave me a burden for Muslims. I began showing them love I hadn't felt before and then found they were more open to me—and to hearing about Jesus Christ."

Dereje pauses a long moment before continuing.

"I graduated during Ramadan and, because of my burden for Muslims, I joined them as they fasted for the thirty days. But while they were fasting for nothing, I was fasting to see them come to know Christ.

"And, praise God, I soon was able to share the gospel with a man from Saudi Arabia, and he gave himself to Christ.

"At that time, in 2016, many people started trusting in Jesus Christ. And that's what led to attacks by angry Muslims the following year."

The students, all young men, lean forward, hanging on Dereje's every word.

"The church where I ministered was destroyed in October 2017," recalls Dereje. "I gathered the believers and shared Psalm 23 with them. We all knew our village would be attacked, and by the time I finished speaking the attack had begun.

"We could hear people being beaten, smell smoke from burning buildings. I ran home as quickly as I could to protect my family."

Dereje describes how Muslims coming to faith in Christ had angered Islamists, who then launched attacks to beat, sexually assault, and kill Christians in an attempt to drive believers from the region. During the riots, more than two thousand homes were destroyed, and a dozen churches—Dereje's among them—leveled.

A knot of angry Muslim extremists arrived at Dereje's front door, screaming for him to come out and face them.

"I grabbed my wife and children and snuck out the back of our house," he says. "We ran, and then watched from a distance as the Islamists destroyed everything we owned.

"We walked for five days," Dereje tells the spellbound students. "Five days walking, each night spent sleeping in the jungle. We had a nine-year-old, five-year-old, and a nine-month-old baby who became so sick we feared she would die. When we finally reached safety, I had to be hospitalized for three days so I could recover.

"For a time we were homeless," Dereje says, "until God brought my family to this mission school compound. Since starting my new role here, five people from a Muslim background have come to faith in Christ. I have Muslim friends who want me to teach them. I've been back to the site of the attacks twice—and am willing to return there to serve if God calls me to do so."

The students watch Dereje carefully, with many likely wondering how he can have a heart for people who would do this to him and his family. Where does he find the courage?

"I've learned to trust the Lord," Dereje tells them. "Just trust the Lord and don't be afraid. Fear is a disease. If you fear, you cannot walk even one step. The one who is with you is greater than fear.

"And I've learned something about sharing the gospel with Muslims," Dereje concludes. "We need to be willing, but it is the Lord who touches their hearts."

And in that moment, the students understand.

God is touching hearts through Dereje not just because he's a gifted speaker who shares words of life. They're drawn to him because he's so fully committed to Christ that he has forgiven those who caused his family pain.

And a love like that is as irresistible as it is fearless.

The students who listened to Dereje learned an unforgettable lesson: the power of forgiveness…not because he lectured about it, or shared Scripture about it, or urged them to do it.

He lived out forgiveness, exemplifying the words of Christ: "But I say to you, Love your enemies and pray for those who persecute you" (Matthew 5:44).

Dereje embodied what Jesus asks us all to become: filled with grace and forgiving, especially to those who wrong us. And what greater demonstration of forgiveness toward his enemies than sharing the gospel with them!

Whom do you need to pray for and forgive today? Is the Holy Spirit leading you to share the gospel with them?

43

EXTREME FORGIVENESS

Susanne Geske and Semse Aydin
Turkey

"Good morning."

"Morning, my friend."

On the sixth floor of an office building in Malatya, a Turkish city of half a million people, Tilman Geske and Necati Aydin greeted each other. They were soon joined by Unger Yuksel, the third partner in their Zirve Christian Publishing business.

Geske, a German national, had lived in Turkey for more than ten years. He was working on a Bible translation project. Aydin, a former Muslim, moved his family to Malatya from elsewhere in Turkey in order to plant a church. Yuksel was a Turkish Christian who had converted from Islam. The men knew that some Turkish nationalists viewed them as enemies who were working to undermine the country's political and religious institutions.

They began their day's work. Later that morning, the trio welcomed five young men, ages nineteen to twenty-one, to their office for a discussion about faith. The meeting had been requested in advance, but a discussion was not what the young men intended. Shortly after the meeting began, they tied up Geske, Aydin, and Yuksel, tortured them, and slit their throats.

The police arrived much too late to intervene. However, all five assailants were eventually apprehended.

The murders were shocking enough; but what stunned the Turkish people was how the wives of two of the murdered men responded. They immediately forgave their husbands' killers.

Soon after mopping her husband's blood from the office floor, Susanne Geske told a reporter, "God, forgive them, for they know not what they do. I forgive the ones who did this."

Later, she explained her response: "I had not had a single second of anger or anything in my heart—nothing. Actually, 'didn't know what they did' is what came to my mind. Because the Lord forgave me so much, so I have forgiven them. Nonbelievers always say, 'How does this work? How do you do that?' I don't do that—this comes from the Lord directly."

In time, Susanne's daughters emulated their mother's response. At first, her oldest daughter was understandably angry, blaming the Turks and wanting to return to Germany. A few months later, however, she asked her mother if they could visit the assassins in prison. She wanted to pray with them, give them a Bible, and share Jesus with them.

Susanne's youngest daughter, then eight, had similar thoughts. "Maybe they can become believers," she said. "And then if they die and come into heaven, they can tell Daddy and Necati and Unger that they are sorry."

Semse, Necati's widow, also was quick to forgive. "I didn't work to try to forgive them," she said. "God just gave me a gift."

She pointed out that forgiveness didn't mean she avoided feeling hurt over losing her husband. "I suffer a lot," she said. "I'm going to suffer until the day I die. But I'm not sorry for moving here. This was the best thing that could happen for Necati. He did a miracle; he did a wonderful thing. He created a very beautiful scenario of his life."

More than nine years after the murders, the five young men who had gone to the publishing house that day were convicted of premeditated murder. Each received three sentences of life in prison. But Semse reminds us that this story is not about earthly justice. "This story is not a drama," she said. "This story is not about death. This story is about victory, gain, encouragement." She has heard about people who have come to know Jesus because of her husband's death.

"I know God showed his love to Turkey, not only on the cross, but by Necati's blood," Semse continued. "And how can I say, 'Why? Why do you give me this suffering or this cross?' I'm just asking God to help me to hold his cross and to lead people to help me hold his cross with me."

Truly our hope lies in Jesus Christ, who forgives and opens heaven's doors for us. Let us rejoice in the forgiveness we see in the examples of Semse, Susanne, and her daughters, and the impact for eternity they have created. May we support them with our prayers for comfort, strength, and encouragement as they hold up the cross of Christ in the face of persecution.

QUESTIONS FOR REFLECTION AND DISCUSSION

FORGIVENESS

1. In our relationship with others, whether friend or foe, the hardest act of obedience to God is often extending forgiveness. Why do you think that is so? What makes expressing forgiveness so difficult?

    a. Have you heard the phrase, "I will forgive, but I won't forget"? Does that mindset describe genuine forgiveness? Why or why not?

    b. How would you describe the forgiveness God offered to you? Was it conditional or unconditional? Was it partial or complete? Did God's forgiveness display the "I will forgive, but I won't forget" mindset? Explain.

    c. Whose stories in this section inspired you to reevaluate your own attitudes and acts of forgiveness? Why?

2. One of the most compelling examples of forgiveness is displayed during the crucifixion. Read Luke 23:32–34.

   a. Did Christ display an "I will forgive, but I won't forget"
   type of forgiveness through his words? Why or why not?

   b. What do you think Jesus meant when he said, "for they
   know not what they do"? How does that inform our own
   forgiveness when wronged by others?

   c. Following the destruction of his home by Islamists, Dereje
   fled, leaving everything he owned to be destroyed. The
   Lord led Dereje to a mission school where he started anew
   in ministry to Muslims.

      i. How could Dereje have a heart for Muslims after
      Islamic extremists caused such utter destruction and
      disruption of his life?

      ii. Read Colossians 3:13. How did Dereje live out the
      forgiveness he had received from Christ?

      iii. How does Dereje's example of forgiveness inspire you
      to forgive someone who has wronged or offended
      you?

3. Forgiving others is often hard work, especially when an appall-
ing act has taken place.

   a. What did you learn from Fenny's story about her ability
   to forgive those whose suicide bombs left her with such
   scars?

   b. What did Fenny say that helps you understand her ability
   to forgive as Christ forgave? To reject bitterness?

c. What would you do, if you were Fenny, meeting face to face with former terrorists?

4. Repeat the Lord's Prayer found in Matthew 6:9–15. (If you are gathered as a family, class, or group, recite it in unison.)

a. Focus on the words in Matthew 6:14–15 for a moment. Recite them again.

   i. Depending upon the translation you are reading, those who trespass or sin against us or who offend us, are those whom we should forgive. Provide examples from your own life when others sinned against you. What did you do?

   ii. What is the condition of our heavenly Father's forgiveness in the second half of verse 14?

   iii. What is the consequence of failing to forgive others in verse 15?

   iv. Do you really believe that is true? Why or why not?

   v. How does your own perspective change regarding the necessity of forgiveness for biblical disciples after reflecting on these verses?

   vi. What is your next step in living out these verses and truly forgiving those who sin against you each day?

Pray

Commit to God that you will pursue forgiveness. Thank him for the example of forgiveness in the lives of those you have read about in this section.

Part VI

FAITHFULNESS

Therefore, my beloved brothers, be steadfast, immovable, always abounding in the work of the Lord, knowing that in the Lord your labor is not in vain.

1 Corinthians 15:58

Anyone who follows Christ faithfully will pay a price for obeying him and holding fast to the truth of God's Word. It doesn't matter if we live in a community controlled by Islamic extremists who want to kill all Christians, or a community where we have the right to practice our faith but are social outcasts if we do so. Jesus knew it would be this way. He knew that the evil one would tempt us to doubt God, to fear circumstances, to choose the easy path over the difficult one—and ultimately to deny Christ and abandon our walk with him.

It is not easy to be a faithful follower of Jesus Christ when:

• Teaching our family, friends, and neighbors
about Jesus can cost us our lives.

- Worshiping with fellow believers invites whole-sale slaughter by Islamic militants.
- Holding fast to our faith in Jesus and refusing to pledge allegiance to any other name result in beatings torture, imprisonment, or death.
- Standing for the truth of what God says in his Word leads to scorn, hatred, and exclusion from our communities because it is not culturally accepted.

Yet God calls all who commit to follow him to be faithful despite those who oppose us. How is this possible? We remain faithful as we focus, trust, and rely on God, who is faithful to be with us and to reward us for all eternity. We also remain faithful as we support and encourage one another to be faithful *together*—as one body of Christ.

As followers of Jesus, we have the great privilege to pursue and serve God; not just as individuals, but as a family, a body of believers. We have an important role in keeping one another focused on what is right and reminding one another of God's faithfulness. As Hebrews 10:23–25a describes, "Let us hold fast the confession of our hope without wavering, for he who promised is faithful. And let us consider how to stir up one another to love and good works, not neglecting to meet together...but encouraging one another."

What happened to followers of Christ when the apostle Paul was in chains is happening all over the world today. "What has happened to me," he wrote, "has really served to advance the gospel." Because of Paul's faithfulness in the face of fear, "most of the brothers...in the Lord...are much more bold to speak the word without fear" (Philippians 1:12, 14).

Our faithfulness to God influences other believers. The faithfulness of one inspires others to remain true to God—to focus their hearts and minds on Jesus and face the temptations, endure the persecution, and risk everything to follow him. Will we stand with the men, women, and children who tenaciously cling to the hope that God will empower them to remain faithful despite the evil done to them? And will we allow their example to inspire us to live as faithful witnesses for Christ?

44

100 PERCENT FOR JESUS

Ali and Rebekah
Iraq

It was March, the time of year when Mosul's insufferable heat had not yet arrived to bake the Iraqi landscape. In the coolness of the morning, the house was still bathed in darkness. Ali, a small man approaching age fifty, looked at his sleeping wife, Rebekah.

They were rearing three children together—Miriam, nineteen; Gabir, seventeen; and Amira, nine. Life had not been easy—not in Ali's line of work—but it had been a good life. God had provided, despite the war a decade earlier, despite the persecution they suffered for believing in Jesus, and despite their low income. Through it all, Ali and Rebekah had weathered trials and had become especially close.

They lived a comfortable yet humble life in the home of Ali's parents. But household peace remained elusive because his Muslim parents were angry he had turned his back on Islam and become a follower of Jesus Christ. And they were especially angry because his family had chosen to follow his steps of faith.

As he did every morning, Ali tacked a handwritten note above the bed. It was a Scripture verse for his wife to start her day: "Unless a grain of wheat falls into the earth and dies, it remains alone; but if it dies, it bears much fruit" (John 12:24).

He walked into the kitchen and, as was his custom, picked up a dog-eared journal he kept near the toaster. Ali looked up as if in thought, then began to write. "I am so full of the Holy Spirit that lives in my heart, that my small body cannot contain the measure of love he has given me."

Later, his family joined him in prayer. "Heavenly Father," he said, head bowed at the small table, "we pray that as I go out today fishing for men that the harvest would be bountiful. We pray that in this place that has turned its back on the good news, you will do a mighty work through me. Instead of facing Mecca, may people for the first time face you and welcome you into their lives. We pray that revival would come to Iraq. We pray that grace would come to Iraq. We pray that love would come to Iraq. Amen."

During the previous three months, Ali had led seven Muslims to Christ. His family also played a role in the men's spiritual development. Ali knew it was not enough to simply watch a man discreetly pray to ask God for forgiveness, acknowledge him as Lord and Savior, and ask Christ to enter his heart.

"He brought the first convert home," Rebekah said, "took out a basin of water, and washed his feet out of reverence and humility to Christ, and as a reminder that he was a servant to all."

Going out each day to evangelize for Jesus in a city where people generally hate Christ was not a boring routine for Ali. It was his lifeblood. "We should go everywhere and tell people about Jesus," Ali told Rebekah. "I need to win one person for Christ a day, 365 days a year." Sometimes he drove to a site overlooking Mosul and, with hands held high, prayed passionately for the lost souls residing below. Ali and his family knew the danger of his commitment.

Days earlier, he had reminded Rebekah of that danger when he shared Acts 21:13 with her: "Then Paul answered, 'What are you doing, weeping and breaking my heart? For I am ready not only to be imprisoned but even to die in Jerusalem for the name of the Lord Jesus.'"

As Mosul came to life and the darkness gave way to light, Ali kissed his wife on the forehead. She bade him goodbye. It was the last time she would see him alive.

While Ali was conversing with a man on a street corner later that day, a car swerved to a stop beside him. Two men grabbed him, shoved him inside the vehicle, and raced away. His captors tortured him for three days and three nights, then shot Ali nine times.

His killers never identified themselves. No one ever asked for ransom money; nor was anyone apprehended, which isn't unusual in such situations. The Mosul police are not inclined to find the murderers of a man who preached Jesus. Clearly, they just wanted to stop him from spreading the gospel.

Wearing the traditional black garb of a widow in mourning, Rebekah said, "I never thought I would be living without my husband. He was my best friend."

Forty days later, as Ali's family and church community gathered to celebrate his life, everyone agreed that Ali would never have stopped sharing the gospel. During his years of evangelism, he had planted countless seeds. He had introduced many converts to Jesus; these converts in turn brought others to Jesus. The ripple effect went on and on. Ali was a faithful disciple of Jesus who made disciples just as Jesus commanded in Matthew 28:19: "Go therefore and make disciples of all nations."

"Sometimes God allows us to go through a difficult time when we lose a loved one," Ali's daughter Miriam said at the celebration. "During these times, he teaches us how to grow in our faith."

The aftershock of Ali's death arrived soon. His grieving parents blamed Rebekah for their son's death. "Your support of his preaching this Jesus was responsible for our son's kidnapping and murder," they told her. They forced Rebekah and her children out of their house.

Nearly destitute, the family of four settled into a one-bedroom apartment in a village outside Mosul. The move separated them from their church community, but Christians who helped the family were surprised by their sense of peace, acceptance, and stability. Gabir worked after school to help support the family. Miriam attended a public university.

But Rebekah's challenges were not over.

After the ISIS invasion of Mosul—and just two years after her husband was martyred—Rebekah and her three children had to flee their home. They climbed into their small vehicle and drove to safety in Erbil, Kurdistan. However, the family hadn't had time to plan or pack, and they had nowhere to go once they arrived in Erbil. They followed a group of Mosul refugees to evangelical churches but learned they were already overcrowded with displaced people.

Rebekah contacted a front-line worker, who was also a close friend of her family. He arranged for her to stay in the offices of a Christian ministry in the city. Rebekah and her three children lost much more than their home; her oldest daughter was unable to take her final exam at the university, meaning she wouldn't receive credit for her work.

Rebekah has carried on, despite her losses. At times she has been overcome with grief over the loss of her husband. On one such occasion, tears filled her eyes when she talked about Ali. However, a smile spread across her face when she described his passion for the Lord.

"I am stronger now in my faith," she said. "Sometimes women want to cling to their husbands. But to love truly is to let them go and let them do what God needs them to do. I have no regrets. Ali died 100 percent for Jesus. The only thing he left us was his heart."

Instead of living for himself and earthly things, Ali faithfully obeyed God. He recognized a far grander purpose to life and death. As he stood firmly for Christ on earth, he never lost sight of heaven and eternity.

Rebekah accepts his death as more than just a personal loss for her and their children. His death served to advance God's kingdom.

Pray for Rebekah and her family—and so many families like them who faithfully serve Christ after their loved ones die serving him. Pray they will experience comfort in God's arms amid their grief as Christ promises in Matthew 5:4: "Blessed are those who mourn, for they shall be comforted." And pray that they, like Ali, will become seeds planted for God's glory that bear much spiritual fruit, serving as God's faithful witnesses.

45

A MISSED TAXI

Baluan, Shokan, and Temir
Central Asia

The three friends stand side by side next to a busy city street choked with traffic. They scan the tangle of cars, carts, and buses looking for a taxi. At last, one appears in the distance. As it darts closer, jockeying for position, the men glance at one another, each waiting for another to hail the cab.

After the taxi passes, empty and with the driver searching for a fare, the men burst out laughing. They realize none of them actually knows how to hail a taxi; city cabs aren't a part of their rural village lives.

This latest adventure is simply one more story cementing their friendship, and they already share so much.

Four years ago, these men didn't even know one another. Now they are more than just friends.

They're family—sharing unbreakable bonds of Christian faith, brotherhood, and discipleship. And their time in the city just reinforced the sweet fellowship they have with each other.

As a teenager, Baluan couldn't have imagined befriending Christians. A student in a *madrassa*, an Islamic religious school, Baluan hated followers of Christ. When his sisters became Christians, he slammed through the house, telling them they were headed to hell for betraying Islam.

Most people in Central Asia are Muslim, but for many it's merely a matter of culture and habit. That wasn't Baluan. He was deeply devoted, calling other Muslims to prayer five times a day from the mosque minaret. His sisters were an embarrassment to their parents—and to him.

But there was something he couldn't deny: his sisters' changed behavior was having an effect.

Baluan was confused by the two different perspectives he was hearing—one from the mosque and the other from his sisters and their husbands.

Which is true? he wondered in his own search for truth. *Whom should I follow—Jesus or Muhammad?*

Baluan, a married man in his twenties, knew it was time he made a choice…but how?

One night he fell to the floor, weeping. "God," he sobbed, "tell me which is the true way: Christianity or Islam?"

When Baluan awoke the next morning he had his answer.

"It's Jesus," he determined. "He's my Lord and Savior."

Wasting no time, Baluan went straight to a friend. "Islam is not true," he said. "Jesus is Messiah, and he is true."

No knives were unsheathed in response, no death threats hammered to his door. But Baluan's friends turned away. Invitations to community events like weddings and funerals stopped coming.

Still, Baluan and his wife, who also became a Christian, faithfully shared the gospel and eventually a small church formed—with Baluan as its pastor. He brought up Jesus in every conversation he could, including with a contractor named Shokan he had hired to build a kitchen.

• • •

Shokan couldn't figure out why his client wanted to pray in the name of God the Father. *My own father isn't a good person*, Shokan thought. *Why would you call God "Father"?* And in Shokan's understanding of Islam, God was someone who punished you for the wrong you did—period. No questions asked! Love wasn't part of the package.

So when Shokan asked Baluan why he prayed like that, the contractor was surprised by Baluan's gentle answer, which he quoted from the *Injil*, or New Testament.

The two-day kitchen job dragged on for two months because of their lengthy conversations about life and religion.

And weeks later, Shokan confessed his faith in Jesus Christ. On his way home that day, Shokan met a crowd leaving the mosque near his house. Fired up with a zeal for God, he stood and loudly declared the gospel.

"I am coming here to talk to you about Jesus," he told the crowd of Muslims. "Jesus, the Son, died for your sin and then he rose, and if you go to the mosque you cannot get saved."

A few days later, secret police came calling. Seeing an opportunity, Shokan shared the message of Christ with them too.

"You must stop sharing the gospel," they told Shokan.

"I can't stop," replied Shokan.

"You can talk about Jesus, but only inside your own home," they said, finally giving in to his persistence.

Shokan knew he had to get creative.

Since his house was the only one in the village with electricity, Shokan bought an antenna so his television set could pick up the national soccer team's matches. Knowing how much his countrymen love soccer, he invited his neighbors to watch the games at his house—but only if they came several hours before the matches started.

Shokan had an instant captive audience for gospel presentations. He preached and then, when the match started, he went to bed, telling his guests to turn off the television when the match ended.

Shokan's faith in Christ transformed him into a new man. He quit beating his wife and gave up smoking and drinking. Every evening he pulled out his Bible and read aloud to his eight-year-old son as his wife listened in.

Eventually, his wife came to faith in Christ, too, as did Shokan's younger brother.

Baluan noticed his friend's passion for evangelism and suggested Shokan move to a nearby village to plant a house church. Shokan accepted the challenge, but at first the reception was chilly.

When neighbors piled up garbage in front of his house, Shokan and his wife quietly cleaned it up. And when those neighbors eventually asked why they seemed so different, Shokan told them about Jesus.

He's now leading a house church of eight believers, with four others close to professing their faith.

• • •

Baluan continued to talk about Jesus in his village and in his workplace. He brought up Christ so often that his Muslim coworkers began calling him "Pope." They warned another coworker, Temir, that Baluan had betrayed Islam and should be avoided.

But Temir was on his own search for truth and started asking Baluan questions about God. Then he asked a Muslim religious leader the same questions so he could compare answers.

Temir even got a copy of the Quran in his own language and laid it and a Bible side by side on a table. For two years, he studied the books and then decided—he'd follow Jesus Christ.

When one of Temir's coworkers asked him a few weeks later if he had become a Christian, he denied it. *I don't have the courage*, he lamented. But the second time the subject came up at work, he was ready. "I am following Jesus," he told them. The news spread quickly.

The company's owner, who was a friend of his father's, warned Temir he could lose his job if he insisted on being a Christian.

Then one day, Temir's father, uncles, and several Islamic clerics confronted him. They surrounded him and shouted accusations.

Feeling calm, Temir eventually raised his voice. "Please, be quiet!" he pleaded with them.

"The New Testament taught me to love my enemies," he told the angry men. "You are all my relatives, my uncles and my father. Even if you don't accept me, I accept you."

Knowing Temir's faith in Christ would bring shame to his family, his father kicked Temir and his wife—who was also a Christian—out of their home. But Temir and his wife weren't alone. They had the prayers and support of their Christian brothers and sisters.

Brothers like Shokan and Baluan.

Brothers who finally wave down a taxi to begin the long journey back to their rural homes in Central Asia. They spend the trip as they always do when they get together: laughing, sharing stories, and praising God who has brought them together…and sharing the gospel with anyone willing to listen.

Faithful friends are a treasure—so Temir, Shokan, and Baluan are rich. They can count on one another as together they count on Christ.

Many believers living in areas of persecution literally owe their lives to one another. From sharing food and shelter, to nursing each other to health after attacks, faithfulness to Christ is fleshed out in their faithfulness to one another. Pray for Baluan, Shokan, Temir, and countless other Christians that they will have deep, meaningful fellowship with members of the body of Christ.

Perhaps you have stories of other believers' faithfulness to you. If possible, reach out and thank them. Let someone know God has used their faithfulness to encourage you.

And ask if they know how to hail a taxi. It would be a great way to share this story of God's faithfulness with them.

46

THE DREAM

Duhra
Egypt

Duhra lay in bed, eyes closed, listening to the clatter and conversations outside her window.

Cairo was awakening to another sweltering day. And Duhra was awakening to another day of school—and deep sadness.

She wished she could hold onto the dream she had while sleeping. There had been a white building, almost like a mosque. But instead of a minaret on top, a cross rose into a bright blue sky.

It had been beautiful…but now was gone.

Duhra sighed, opened her eyes, and stepped into her day.

Thus far, her life had been anything but easy. When her older sister was born, her father named the little girl "Enough" because he wanted no more daughters. He had had enough! Then Duhra came along, and her father's response was to abandon his wife and children.

Duhra's mother blamed her for the failed marriage and financial pressures that came with feeding a family. So when her mother found a job abroad, she left Duhra, who was still in elementary school, in the care of Duhra's grandmother.

Her grandmother, a devout Muslim, forced Duhra to cover her head and to pray regularly.

Those prayers came easily to Duhra. "I need a mother and father," she kept reminding Allah.

And then came the dream.

Though Duhra had never seen a white building like the one in her dream, she knew about crosses. Her Coptic Christian classmates had crosses tattooed on their wrists or hands, reminders of their Orthodox faith and Christian heritage.

As the days pressed on, Duhra often replayed the dream in her mind. Seeing the building gave her comfort, so she began drawing a cross on one wrist—a cross her grandmother eventually saw.

"How can you betray your faith?" her grandmother demanded. "Don't you know Christians can hurt you? That they do awful things?"

Her grandmother scrubbed Duhra's arm clean and then marched her to a mosque to receive corrective "treatment." The imams' treatment was stern and, to Duhra's horror, turned into sexual assault.

One day, Duhra took a wrong turn while walking home from school. As she glanced around to get her bearings, she saw it: the white building—exactly like the one in her dream—stood at the end of the block. It had the same gleaming façade, the same shining doors, the same cross stretching up into the sky.

Duhra knew not to tell her grandmother what happened, but she couldn't ignore it either. She began secretly visiting a church near her grandmother's house.

When Duhra turned thirteen, her grandmother died, forcing her mother to return to Egypt to care for her "problem child." Her mother already resented Duhra and, when she discovered Duhra was involved with a church, that anger and abuse intensified.

Duhra was even shoved out of the house at night, forced to sleep in the dirt by a nearby bus station. But despite her punishments, she was still drawn to Christ and his church.

At fifteen, Duhra's family moved, and she discovered their new neighbor was a Christian. He introduced her to a Coptic priest who gave Duhra a Bible and began teaching her about the Christian faith.

The more Duhra learned, the better she understood how God had been reaching out to her all along. She placed her faith in Christ and felt something she'd long wanted: love. But even as peace flooded her soul, the mistreatment at home continued.

Duhra's mother beat her so often that she finally hired off-duty police officers to do the beating when she was too tired to continue. She dragged Duhra to the National Security Office for even more "correction."

Duhra was perpetually bruised and scratched, and at one point both her legs were broken. Even now, fifteen years after the torture ceased, Duhra experiences pain in her legs. Because she never received medical treatment, the bones set awkwardly; the pain will be with her the rest of her life.

Duhra's mother finally found a way to be rid of her daughter when Duhra turned twenty-one. She arranged a marriage between Duhra and a strict Muslim man who promised to bring Duhra to Islam—whatever it took.

When he found a cross tattooed on his new wife's shoulder, he poured acid on her back to burn away the offending symbol. The searing pain brought Duhra to her knees as acid blistered and then ate through her skin.

Kept as a wounded prisoner in her home, Duhra was isolated from the loving encouragement of her church family, support she'd never needed more.

When Duhra and her husband had a son, she gave the boy a Christian name. In response, her husband beat and divorced her, then shoved her out onto the street…without her son.

Duhra now awakens with a new dream: seeing and holding her child. When she filed a legal complaint, the court ruled that, because she's a Christian, she has no parental rights. Christian converts from Islam have zero legal protection and are viewed as having little value.

When employers learn of her Christian faith, she's dismissed or abused. One employer withheld her wages for three years and now refuses to pay her, knowing she has no legal recourse.

But Duhra isn't alone. Her church family stands with her and provides housing and emotional support. There's also some financial help with her many medical bills, a legacy of the beatings she took for remaining faithful to Christ.

"I never sensed the meaning of having a family," she explains. "I only felt it in the church; the place where I have joy is only in the church."

And in spite of the pain, Duhra also finds joy in the challenges she's faced.

"God is really with me," she says. "I think all the suffering and struggles…strengthened me and gave me an indication that I am on the right path."

The scars on Duhra's back are a reminder of her ex-husband's attempt to erase her faith in Christ. The peace in her heart—peace even in the midst of heartbreak—is a reminder he didn't succeed.

Losing a child—for any reason—cuts so deeply the pain defies description. And it's pain Duhra feels daily because she's chosen to remain faithful to Christ.

The scars on her back ache. The throbbing in her legs nearly cripples her. But losing her son is agony and sends her to God for comfort and understanding.

Like David, the Psalmist, Duhra's heart cries out, "Hide not your face from me.…O you who have been my help…For my father and my mother have forsaken me, but the Lord will take me in. Teach me your way, O Lord, and lead me on a level path because of my enemies" (Psalm 27:9–11). God's love has sustained and guided Duhra and will sustain and guide you when the cost of your faithfulness is high.

Because you're not alone either. Not now, not ever.

47

FIGHTING AGAINST GOD

Shahnaz and Ebi
Iran

In his apartment high above a northern Iranian city, Ebi angrily clenched and unclenched his fists. *How could my daughter do this to me?*

"Shahnaz," he said, turning to her, "you are just going through a phase. It is like your fascination with this Islamic prophet or that American musician."

"Father, that is not true," she answered. "I am a Christian. I am a follower of Jesus—a passionate follower of Jesus!"

His heart pounded faster. *I must remain calm.* He tried to convince himself that it was only a passing fad. After all, young people were so impressionable, and two-thirds of Iran's population was under age thirty. What would fascinate them next?

"My daughter," he stated carefully, "I am confident you will soon leave this passing fancy behind, as you have your other fascinations with the West."

"No," she said, "this is different. This is not of the mind. This is of the heart."

Ebi bit his bottom lip lightly. "I am not requesting this, Shahnaz. I am *demanding* this. I am your father! You will not shame me, our family, or Allah by embracing a myth we despise. You will leave this Jesus behind you!"

"Father, are you listening to me?" she replied. "For the first time in my life, I am *content!*"

He clenched his fists and kept them clenched. *How dare she turn against the faith that I steeped her in! How dare she risk humiliating me!*

He said nothing and did nothing. But for two years, Ebi grew angrier—angrier when he learned his daughter associated with a group of young people who studied the Bible, and angrier when he discovered she was telling her friends about this Jesus.

Then he and his wife came up with a plan. They would fight Shahnaz's obsession with this Jesus by tempting her with love. Before she had been duped into this conspiracy against Allah, she had been in love with a young Muslim living nearby. They forbade her from marrying him, even though she desperately wanted him as her husband. Perhaps yesterday's problem would be today's solution, her parents surmised.

They invited the young man and his parents to their apartment to discuss a possible marriage. When Shahnaz learned they had lied about her renewed interest in the man, she cried and became angry. She no longer loved this man, nor did she want to marry him. She also didn't want to embarrass him or his parents.

So she asked to speak with her father privately. "I'm sorry, Father," she told him, "but I am a Christian now. I cannot marry a Muslim. My life has changed. I have a goal to serve God. And you, Father, would be well to serve him too. He is different than Allah. He—"

"Enough!" Ebi spit out harshly.

When they realized Shahnaz had rejected their son, the parents left with him in a huff. Now Shahnaz's parents were embarrassed. "How dare you shame us like this!" her father shouted when their guests left.

As his wife walked briskly to another room, Ebi unfastened his belt, yanked it from his pants, and whipped it across his daughter's back.

Whack. She collapsed to the floor.

"Do you realize that I can kill you right now, and it is legal?" he raged. "You are a Muslim who has become a Christian! You are an apostate! My reputation will be ruined because of you!"

Shahnaz cowered as he struck her again, and again, and again.

"I am going to keep beating you until you get on your knees and renounce Christianity and return to Islam," he shouted. Sweat gleamed on Ebi's face as he panted for breath.

"Lord," Shahnaz cried out, "I do not want to deny my faith. Jesus, help me!"

As her father raised the belt to hit her again, something strange happened. As if guided by some unseen force, he stretched his arm wide to the side and began whipping himself in the face.

Whack! Whack! Whack!

"Father?"

"I am a...bad...person," he said softly, his voice no longer laced with anger. "I am so dirty. I am so stupid. I am fighting with God."

Shahnaz watched in amazement at the puzzling miracle unfolding in front of her.

Her father fell forward on the floor. "Please forgive me, God," he prayed, tears streaming down his face.

Shahnaz's mother raced into the room when she heard his body fall. "What did you do? Kill him?" she screamed.

"Mother," Shahnaz replied, "I don't know what happened."

Her mother started punching the emergency number into her cell phone.

Ebi's eyes suddenly opened, and with great effort he stood to his feet. "I do not need an ambulance," he said. "I know now what I really need."

He stepped toward Shahnaz, who instinctively stepped back. But he opened his arms—and wrapped his daughter in an embrace. His wife stared in astonishment. Shahnaz felt the unexpected assurance that she was safe.

"Please forgive me," her father said. "Now I realize who I am fighting against."

Ebi then told her about a vision. "As I was beating you, I saw Jesus with his left arm wrapped around you. With his right arm he motioned me to stop the whipping. He said to me, 'Stop beating her. She belongs to me.' I realized as I was swinging the belt that I was beating Jesus."

Weeks later—after many discussions with Shahnaz and other believers about the Jesus his daughter would not cast aside—Ebi humbled himself and placed his trust in Jesus Christ. Now as he looked down on the city from his apartment, Ebi experienced the peace of God—a peace he'd never felt before and still could not fully understand.

He glanced at his watch. It was time to get ready. Guests would be arriving soon for the church meeting he and his wife had offered to host.

Christ promised his disciples power through the Holy Spirit "in Jerusalem and in all Judea and Samaria, and to the end of the earth" (Acts 1:8). And Shahnaz experienced the Holy Spirit's power to be Christ's witness in her own home—even relying on the Holy Spirit's power when her own father was beating her. The fruit of her faithfulness to Christ led to Ebi's salvation. Praise God!

Today, lift up Christians like Shahnaz who are persecuted by family members. Pray that they will stand firm in the Lord, experiencing his power to be his witnesses. Pray that, like Ebi, their family members who oppose their faith will be won to Christ through their faithful witness.

48

LOSING FAMILY, FINDING CHRIST

Alejandro
The Philippines

Alejandro looked in the mirror hanging in his bamboo hut. He liked what he saw. The only son in a strict Muslim family, he grinned as he considered how he had honored his father by joining Islamic rebels. Now he had become a cold-blooded killer, a terrorist for Allah. He even killed Christians. *My killing*, he thought, *proves that I am a worthy heir.*

Little did he know that one day he'd look in that same mirror in shame, no longer viewing his violent actions so proudly. "I was not afraid to kill anyone for the glory of Allah," he recalled. "It was easier to kill a person than a chicken."

Even killers have a conscience, and Alejandro's Christ-driven guilt finally made its way into his soul. Although he remained committed to his Muslim faith and family, he left the militant

289

group and turned to secular work. He hoped to find satisfaction in comfort and pleasure.

Jesus once again tugged on his heart. A Christian man he had met during his travels around the island of Mindanao—one of 7,000 Philippine islands—invited him to church. Alejandro initially declined, yet the invitations persisted so he finally said yes. At church, God shattered the mirror image Alejandro had of himself. He saw what he really was: a cold-blooded murderer seeking satisfaction through violence, power, and bullying. It was as if God were saying, "See yourself as I see you; as a sinner, yes, but as a sinner saved by my grace."

For the first time since he was a little boy, Alejandro crumpled into tears. "I was a tough military guy, an Islamic killer," he said. "I never cried."

That day he decided to leave Islam and follow Jesus.

When Alejandro told his father of his conversion, the man exploded angrily and waved a machete in his son's face. "A curse on you!" he seethed. "I will *kill* you!"

Alejandro fled from the family home and has not seen his parents since that day. Occasionally, he talks with his siblings, and they always tell him the same thing: their parents still feel angry, wounded, and betrayed.

Alejandro wasn't about to sacrifice his new love for Jesus Christ in order to reconcile with his parents. He had received a new life and an eternal perspective of his purpose for living. He quit his job and enrolled in Bible school.

Four years later, when Alejandro completed his degree, leaders of the denomination who hired him sent him to a remote, abandoned church building. At one time, 130 families had worshiped there. That is, until relentless attacks by Muslim extremists drove them away.

To say that he faced daunting challenges to remain faithful would be a drastic understatement. The situation in the area did not improve immediately. His life was at risk each day. At night he wore earplugs to block the sounds of gunfire and exploding grenades as rebels, just as he had once been, attacked nearby villages.

When Alejandro traveled to neighboring villages to share the good news of Jesus, he walked or rode a water buffalo. It was a humbling change from his terrorist missions when he led raids racing in on a truck or motorcycle. Through all the challenges, Alejandro remained faithful. The church body began to grow a little at a time.

While attending a Christian conference, Alejandro met other persecuted pastors. Those interactions renewed and refreshed him. He even experienced the joy of leading a Muslim to Christ. During the final evening of the conference, Alejandro spoke extensively with an attendee grieving the loss of relatives—a pastor, his wife, and children—who had been killed by Muslim militants several months earlier.

Only God could bring together a former Muslim murderer of Christians to comfort and pray for believers who were suffering at the hands of Islamic extremists.

Alejandro, who has dedicated his life to sharing the gospel, experiences daily the challenge the apostle Paul gave to followers of Christ at Colossae: "Set your minds on things that are above, not on things that are on earth. For you have died, and your life is hidden with Christ in God" (Colossians 3:2–3). The old Alejandro is dead, and his new life is in Christ.

Pray for him, and for all who follow Christ, to be faithful to the new vision of ourselves that only God can give. Only God can transform a life built on hate into one built on the eternal foundation of Jesus Christ and his love.

49

A FAMILY ON MISSION

Zamira and Atamurat
Uzbekistan

The harsh pounding on the door could only mean one visitor: police.

This wasn't the first time the apartment had been raided. The government was suspicious of Zamira and her husband, Atamurat, because of their Christian faith and work.

Waving a search warrant at Zamira, the policeman and his colleagues ignored Uzbekistan's custom of removing shoes when entering the house. Cowering in a corner of the living room, Zamira and her three sons watched the intruders empty drawers, cabinets, and search through closets looking for Christian materials.

The raids never got any easier for Zamira, especially when her husband was away. The stress was taking a toll on her health, causing depression and weight loss.

One policeman examined a family photo hanging on the wall, a portrait made before the raids and threats began. He then looked Zamira up and down.

"You're pale and skinny," he sneered. "You must be sick."

Having made a mess of the apartment, the men prepared to leave—but not before the police officer issued a warning.

"All you have to do is be like everybody else," he said. "Nobody would come and disturb you like this."

As Christians, Zamira and Atamurat were aware they stood out from other Uzbeks, most of whom are Muslim and consider biblical Christians a fringe sect.

And Zamira knew the police officer wasn't making a request, but an order to stop practicing Christianity—one she and her husband were not intending to follow.

• • •

Zamira became a Christian through the witness of her mother, who heard about Christ when she was working in Russia. While a teenager, Zamira prayed she'd find a Christian husband; but in Uzbekistan, where would she find such a man? She knew of no other Christians in her town.

During her second year of university, Zamira met a Muslim classmate named Atamurat. As she and her fellow students picked cotton—something required at most schools in Uzbekistan—she daydreamed about him. Atamurat was just what she was looking for with one notable problem: he didn't know Jesus.

One afternoon, as Zamira worked in the cotton fields, she looked up to see Atamurat approaching on horseback. He smiled, reached down, and pulled her up onto the horse.

Now that she had his full attention, Zamira took the opportunity to share the gospel with him as they rode. But Atamurat was skeptical. He stayed dubious for more than two years as Zamira prayed for him and continued sharing about Jesus Christ.

When Atamurat finally placed his faith in Christ, Zamira married him the next week.

Following graduation, the couple spent a year at a Bible school before returning to their hometown. Starting with the Gospel of Matthew, Atamurat began translating the Bible from Russian into their native language, Karakalpak. Sharing the gospel with their friends and family came naturally to Zamira and Atamurat. Translating the Bible brought them an excitement for learning they couldn't keep to themselves. And some friends and family did place their trust in Christ.

In time, Atamurat and Zamira formed a small house church, which grew to thirty members. For four years they seemed to go unnoticed by authorities. But when government persecution of Christians intensified in the area, meeting together came with consequences.

Police raided Christian meetings, confiscating cellphones and laptops, before hauling Christians to police headquarters for hours of interrogation. Church leaders were fined. And Zamira and Atamurat knew they were being watched.

The increased surveillance prompted Atamurat and other leaders to switch tactics. They changed the location of their meetings each week, sharing the next meeting place by word of mouth.

One Sunday morning the house church had no place to gather. "Lord, where do you want to meet your bride today?" Atamurat prayed. His prayer was answered when one of the church members called.

"I had a birthday three days ago," she said, using their code language. "Please come."

That day, eighteen church members met in her home. But the moment worship started, police burst in. Searching the home and finding a Bible lesson on the printer, officers arrested everyone and took them to police headquarters.

As the Christians waited their turn to be interviewed, they resumed singing how Jesus will overcome, a fitting song in their circumstances. They even managed to take up an offering.

This is the place you prepared for us to worship! Atamurat said to the Lord as he remembered his earlier prayer.

Atamurat, Zamira, and the house church Christians were released. But what they didn't know was that was the beginning of a ten-year stretch of persecution for the couple.

The raids on Atamurat and Zamira's home became more frequent. And they struggled to support church members facing the same social and family pressures. Added to the couple's stress was raising three sons who witnessed and experienced the persecution with them.

One day, the persecution came to a head. Police raided the house church and arrested all four families in attendance, including Atamurat and Zamira. Prayer requests found on the apartment walls were enough evidence for the authorities to fine everyone. In fact, they fined them forty times the normal amount for illegal meetings, and the men were sentenced to fifteen days in prison.

The warden greeted Atamurat and the three new prisoners with a stern lecture. "You betrayed your faith," he told them.

The men were led to their cells. Atamurat was placed in a small cell with a member of a banned Islamist group who had never met an Uzbek Christian.

Atamurat seized the opportunity and shared stories about Jesus with the man. Standing up and pacing the room, his Muslim cellmate was curious and asked numerous questions. "What is clean food, and what is unclean?" he asked Atamurat.

"It is not what goes into the mouth that defiles the person, but what comes out of the mouth; this defiles the person," Atamurat replied, referring to the words of Christ in Matthew chapter 15.

When the two cellmates received their once-daily meal, Atamurat thanked God for the food and the hands that prepared it. By the third day, his Muslim cellmate volunteered to pray, repeating what he had heard Atamurat say and closing with "in the name of Jesus."

The gospel was taking hold.

Each evening a Muslim teacher came to preach Islam to the four Christians. Deciding that one in particular was likeliest to recant his Christian faith, the warden had prison guards beat the man until he was covered with bruises.

Three times the warden called Atamurat to the prison office. And each time, Atamurat prayed for God to give him the right words to say. During one visit, the warden asked if the pastor was confident he'd be going to paradise.

"Yes, I am 100 percent sure," Atamurat responded confidently.

The warden's eyes narrowed. "I have attended mosque for twenty years," he said, "and I know every major spiritual leader in the area. None of them can say he is 100 percent sure. How in the world can you say that?"

"Because Muhammad never made a promise," Atamurat answered and then explained that only Jesus gave the promise that whoever believes in him will be with him in paradise.

On the last day of Atamurat's sentence, the warden called him to the office one last time. On the desk sat three Bibles: one in Russian, one in Uzbek, and one in the local Karakalpak language.

The warden pointed to the Bibles. "You four say Jesus is the Son of God," the warden said, "but that's not in the Bible."

"It is," Atamurat replied, and showed him 1 John chapter 1.

The warden sighed. "This is why we don't give church registration to you. If we do, many people will want to join you."

Soon after Atamurat was released from prison, he, Zamira, and their sons traveled to a neighboring country for a time of rest. Zamira and the children recovered from the trauma of his brief imprisonment, and Atamurat received clarity about whether he had done anything wrong. While he was sitting in jail—and for a while after his release—he wondered what he should have done differently to prevent being arrested and put in jail. But God's answer was clear: he had done nothing wrong. In fact, God had made sure he was in the right place at the right time.

Atamurat had been faithful—and that was exactly what God wanted.

Atamurat was one of the last Christians in Uzbekistan to be imprisoned for his faith. Although restrictions on Christians decreased significantly, many converts from Islam still cope with persecution from family members, society, and even the government.

Atamurat's church was eventually granted official registration and soon afterward received an unexpected gift. A group of foreign Christians who had been denied registration years earlier gifted Atamurat their long-vacant church building. Included are pews, a sound system, and everything needed for the growing congregation.

"It's like a promised land," Atamurat said. And not only does his congregation meet there, but also two other congregations worship there.

Atamurat and Zamira still share a steady, faithful witness. In addition to their work with the church, Atamurat leads a sports ministry, praying with the players before each match in the name of Jesus. And Zamira opened a makeup studio in her home, using the opportunity to gently share her faith with women.

Even their three sons inject the gospel into every interaction with others.

It's still sometimes dangerous to do Christian work, but that doesn't deter the family. They've seen the fruit that comes with faithfully following Christ—it's growing all around them.

And it's blossoming in them as well.

Pray for Atamurat and Zamira and others like them—their faithfulness has kept them in a place where honoring Christ comes at a cost. Pray that God will raise up faithful men and women through the fruit of their ministry (2 Timothy 2:2).

But also thank God for them. Their lives tell the story of what faithfulness can bring, the fulfillment that comes with walking on that narrow path of obedience.

Obedience travels hand in hand with faithfulness. It's what faithfulness looks like when fleshed out in daily life.

So pray for them. And pray your faithfulness can inspire others, too.

50

THE IRRESISTIBLE POWER OF LOVE

Ehsan
Iraq

In the northern city of Erbil, a dry and dusty wind only worsened the pungent stench of burning trash and smoke from nearby industries. The smell of outdoor cooking announced another day unfolding in this gathering spot of refugees from war and violence. A mass of people sought shade in church courtyards and half-built or abandoned buildings. On the street, people propped up plastic, cardboard—anything—to shelter them from the scorching heat of the relentless sun.

Less than an hour's drive separates the better-known city, Mosul, from Erbil. Mosul is a conservative, Arab-majority city with a strong Islamist flavor. Erbil is a moderate Kurdish city that hosts refugees from all over the region: Arab Iraqis, Persians, Kurdish Iranians, and Syrians.

Amid this setting, Azhar prayed silently before he gently brought up the subject of Jesus to his Muslim friend, Ehsan. He had talked with Ehsan about Jesus before, but his friend had resisted the gospel.

"How can God, as you say, be both fully human and fully God?" Ehsan asked. Azhar tried to explain the concept, but his answer didn't satisfy Ehsan, who then brought up other concerns. "Christians killed Muslims in the name of religion during the Crusades, and the Christians I know are hypocrites. They preach lives of purity and live lives of impurity."

Azhar knew well the Bible's warning about hypocrites and how Jesus had exposed the hypocrisy of the Pharisees and others whose walk didn't match their talk.

"The Bible, on which our faith rests, condemns the very immorality you speak of," replied Azhar. "Not everyone who calls himself a Christian is a true believer."

Ehsan shrugged his shoulders, unconvinced, and their conversation shifted to another topic.

Azhar continued to pray for his friend as a new level of immorality swept into the region like a plague. Jihadis from the Islamic State overran Mosul in their attempt to establish a purely Islamic political-religious state. The jihadis gave Christians who lived in Mosul an ultimatum: convert to Islam, pay a high tax that virtually nobody could afford, leave the city, or be killed.

Many Christ-followers fled to nearby Iraqi Kurdistan, where Christian workers were already busy helping Syrian refugees and Iraqis who had been displaced during earlier conflicts. Others fled to Erbil. Amid the chaos and despair, Azhar and other believers did what God called them to do: serve others. They worked tirelessly to meet the needs of refugees in the region. As part of that effort, they stuffed plastic bags with food, clothing, hygiene items, and Bibles before distributing them to desperately needy people.

For two months, Ehsan, who had an office job, watched from afar. "Ehsan," asked Azhar one day, "would you like to help?"

Ehsan hesitated, then agreed to lend a hand. The team of volunteers worked for nine hours without even stopping to eat lunch. When they finished, Azhar invited Ehsan to join him for dinner. Midway through the meal, Azhar noted something different in Ehsan's disposition. It came to light when Ehsan asked, "What kind of love do you have? What's the reason for this love?"

Surprised by the question, Azhar didn't reply immediately, thinking his friend might have further questions.

"Why do you include Bibles in these bags?" Ehsan continued. "And how can you love people you don't even know?"

Realizing that Ehsan's involvement with refugees had deepened his curiosity, Azhar replied, "Today you saw that there is a God who empowered us to work hard all day. He is the one who gives us this love." Ehsan kept asking questions about the source of this love. Then he asked one more question Azhar had not expected: Could he have a Bible?

"I suggest you start reading in Matthew," Azhar said, handing a Bible to his friend. "If you get stuck on something you don't understand, pray and ask Jesus for answers. Call me in the morning, and tell me about what you read."

The next morning, Azhar kept checking the time, eager to hear from Ehsan. But no call came. Worried, Azhar finally called him.

"My friend," Ehsan stated slowly, with conviction, "I have been up the whole night. Jesus revealed himself to me. I want to take the final step. I want to be baptized. I want to get involved in ministry like you."

When they met again, Azhar embraced his new brother in Christ and taught him all he could about the Christian faith. "There is no halfway commitment," Azhar emphasized. "The Christian life is a life of sacrifice."

Ehsan seemed to understand. He began attending a small house church in Erbil and was baptized. He continued to help pack supplies for the refugees. He prayed with those who received them.

Months later, a coworker of Ehsan's approached Azhar, knowing that he was Ehsan's friend. "What's different about Ehsan?" he asked. "There's a change, a new peace there."

"I'll tell you the reason," answered Azhar, knowing that Ehsan would want the truth shared. "He knows Jesus now."

Azhar invited the coworker to the weekly worship meeting. The man came and, as the meeting ended, asked, "Could I have a Bible?"

Sometimes the need underlying people's questions about faith and the Bible isn't about finding answers and dealing with theology. It's about seeing the sincere love of Christ demonstrated in places where that love is greatly needed. When biblical disciples take the gospel message seriously and live out God's love in their relationships, people who need him can't help but notice. Jesus said that his love would make a difference: "By this all people will know that you are my disciples, if you have love for one another" (John 13:35).

It is our actions, not just our words, that cause people who do not know Christ to ask questions and respond. Ehsan had heard the gospel many times, but it was actions that demonstrated the love of Jesus that moved him to believe. Love in action powerfully draws people to the source of that love: God through his Word.

May God's love so fill our hearts that it will be evident in how we serve and care for others.

51

SEEKING AND FINDING IN BANGLADESH

Pintu Hossain
Bangladesh

Pintu Hossain stood in front of the little brick church. In many ways, he felt like Joseph, the man he had read about in a Bible course, a man exiled by his brothers. Thrown into a well. Alone. Abandoned. Hopeless. Yet Pintu was surrounded by crowds of people, a reminder that Bangladesh is the most densely populated and poorest country in the world.

Pintu felt his heart pounding. *All these people going here and there*, he thought. *Where are they going? Why am I following them?* Then his mind switched to even more pressing questions: *Should I walk into this church? What about all the questions I've wrestled with since I was a child?*

In a country where nearly nine out of ten people are Muslim, Pintu had grown up believing Islam was the only true religion. He prayed five times a day. He fasted for thirty days during Ramadan. He encouraged others to pray with him in the mosque. *Why*, he wondered, *don't I feel content? Why am I not satisfied with my faith? Why haven't all my prayers and fasting assured me that I am right in following the masses?*

During high school, Pintu had been fascinated by the idea of learning from people outside his culture. He began writing letters, hoping that recipients would write back. Some did. Corresponding with them became a serious hobby.

"Pintu," said a friend, "here is someone to whom you should write."

Its name, the Bible Correspondence Course, puzzled Pintu. *What is this Bible? What is this course? Is this the stuff of that Christian religion, the religion of idolaters who worship three different gods instead of Allah?*

But the offer, he had to admit, intrigued him. If he completed the Bible course, he would receive a free Bengali Bible. "Dear sir," he began, "please sign me up for your course. I would like to take it."

When the Bible course arrived, its stories only deepened his concerns about Islam. Here was a Christian God purporting to have created all people, to love all people, and to forgive them even when they sin. Pintu completed the course in nine months and, as promised, received the Bible. Family members became angry when they noticed what he was reading. Just as Joseph's brothers abandoned him, Pintu's siblings turned their backs on him. They believed he was being unfaithful to Islam.

Still, Pintu wrestled with deeper questions about life and God. He went to a local imam and asked, "Can Muhammad truly save me?"

The imam furrowed his brow. "What? Are you doubting our prophet?"

Pintu decided he would search for answers in the Quran. He didn't find any.

Finally, longing for truth and feeling curious, he stood in front of that little church, a tranquil point in a world teeming with motion. He opened the door and entered, then quickly regretted it. The man in front, who seemingly had just started his talk, abruptly stopped speaking. The few dozen people in the room looked concerned.

The man started speaking again, from the beginning, but immediately stopped again. Now people began whispering.

For a third time, the man started speaking, and for a third time he stopped.

He is a crazy man! Pintu thought, retreating to the door in a huff. He had just opened it when the man spoke again, and his words went straight to Pintu's heart.

"I apologize," the man told the small congregation, "but each time I start the message, I keep sensing that God wants me to talk about another subject. About someone from the Old Testament. About Joseph, a man who was exiled by his brothers."

Pintu let go of the doorknob. He slowly turned around. *Joseph?* He returned to his seat, eyes riveted on the speaker.

As the man talked about Joseph and his brothers' betrayal, Pintu listened with increasing amazement. *This man is telling my story!* As soon as the meeting ended, Pintu rushed up to the speaker. "Do you know me?"

The pastor said he didn't.

"Then how do you know my life story?" Pintu asked.

Something clicked in the speaker's mind. "Now I understand why God did not allow me to preach my prepared sermon," he answered. "Today was a very special service, and I have been preparing for preaching a good sermon. But I heard a whispering sound in my ears, saying, 'Don't preach this sermon. Instead, preach from the life of Joseph.'"

Three times the voice had come to him, whenever he began his prepared sermon. Finally, he obeyed the voice.

"Now I understand it is because of you," he said, smiling at Pintu. "God has brought you here to give you a new life through Jesus."

Pintu and the pastor talked for two more hours, discussing questions that had plagued the young man for so long. Slowly, he came to understand the truth about Jesus. He bowed his head and prayed for salvation.

When his parents learned of his decision, they kicked him out of their home. But Pintu remained faithful to Jesus. He prayed fervently for opportunities to share the gospel with them and the siblings who had abandoned him. One by one, each came to Christ.

Without knowing it, Pintu had experienced this promise of Jesus: "Ask, and it will be given to you; seek, and you will find; knock, and it will be opened to you" (Matthew 7:7). He had been faithful to keep "knocking" and "seeking" spiritual hope. He sought God. He completed the study course. He walked into that church. Despite his uncertainty, he took those steps of faith—and God changed his life forever.

Now Pintu reaches out to Muslims who feel alone, abandoned, and hopeless, and who are looking for something more to life—just like Pintu did.

It is a great privilege for followers of Christ to walk with those who seek to know God. May we be faithful to continue seeking him and to obey his "whispering" in our ears.

52

"IF TODAY IS THE DAY I'M KILLED"

Ibrahim
Kenya

Ibrahim looked at the blank piece of paper and gripped his pen.

If anything happens to me, he wrote, *my chief and my clan have eliminated me.*

Ibrahim folded the letter and tucked it into an envelope. He then strapped an old service revolver to his belt, straightened his robe, and closed the door behind him.

He was heading to his baptism. And, perhaps, his martyrdom.

As a young man, Ibrahim could never have imagined becoming a Christian. He'd been born into the Ogaden tribe, a powerful Somali clan who lived in Somalia, Kenya, and Ethiopia. Like all male clan members, he was raised not only to be a good Muslim, but also to be a Muslim leader.

So he enrolled in a *madrassa,* an Islamic religious school, with the aim of becoming an imam. After two years of training, Ibrahim was zealously going door-to-door to persuade others to convert to Islam when his plans were abruptly derailed.

World War II was dragging on and the British needed more fighters. Their solution was to draft young men from their colonies—and one such colony was Ibrahim's native Kenya. Though units were initially segregated by religion, the realities of war meant regiments were eventually combined. For the first time, Ibrahim was with non-Muslims, even eating from the same plates with them—unthinkable for most devout Muslims.

Ultimately, he came to accept them as friends and brothers-in-arms. It was the first time Ibrahim had accepted the idea that a non-Muslim could be a good person.

When the war ended, Ibrahim was one of fifty ethnic Somalis accepted into a police training program in Mombasa, Kenya. After graduating, he eagerly joined the force.

Ibrahim was in uniform the day he first heard the gospel, on duty observing a large crowd listening to a Christian missionary. His commander feared the event might trigger an attack, so Ibrahim stood scanning the crowd, alert for any sudden movements.

When the missionary opened a Bible and began reading from Exodus 14, Ibrahim was surprised to hear a familiar story about the Israelites fleeing Egypt.

At first Ibrahim thought the missionary was reading from the Quran, which also tells of the same event.

Why is a Christian reading from a Muslim holy book? Ibrahim wondered. *Is he Muslim or Christian?*

Ibrahim's curiosity about the sermon and its source led him to visit a church not far from the police encampment where he slept each night. He arranged to meet with the church's pastor.

"Why was your missionary speaking out of the Quran?" Ibrahim asked the pastor. He discovered that, yes, some events were described in both the Quran and the Bible.

Ibrahim asked which versions were written first. He figured the oldest would be most accurate as it was written nearest to the time of the event. To his surprise, Ibrahim learned the Bible's Exodus account came first and was attributed to Moses—an actual eyewitness.

The pastor handed Ibrahim a Bible and, still the scholar of his younger years, Ibrahim dug in. He found that while the Quran talks about Jesus (Isa), the Bible paints a fuller picture using accounts written by people who actually walked and talked with him—and who witnessed his miracles firsthand.

Ibrahim felt his childhood faith crumbling and his life transitioning—in more ways than one.

He left the police force and took a bookkeeping job in Nairobi, Kenya. Ibrahim no longer felt bound by the Quran, but he wasn't yet ready to accept Jesus as the Son of God. Doing so would mean turning his back on his family, clan, and culture.

He felt adrift, but soon realized he wasn't alone.

An accountant working alongside Ibrahim was also an assistant pastor. When he noticed Ibrahim exploring God's Word, he offered to meet with his colleague for Bible study. Ibrahim bombarded the pastor with questions as they studied, and his coworker patiently answered each one.

Eventually Ibrahim accepted his friend's invitation to attend church. In time he placed his faith in Jesus Christ and was baptized—the first time.

Ibrahim's wife, Habiba, cried each time he walked into the room. Her friends urged her to leave him; for a time she took their advice, moving back to her father's house.

Leaders in Ibrahim's clan were equally upset. "No one in our clan has done this before!" they protested, reminding Ibrahim that no one in their tribe had ever abandoned Islam. The clan chief even offered a bribe: 400 cows, 200 camels, a large tract of land, and his daughter in marriage—but only if Ibrahim renounced Christ.

Ibrahim refused. "I have never seen faith that is bought," he told them.

Clan elders ratcheted up the pressure and this time threatened him with physical harm. "If I hear you are still a Christian," the Ogaden chief told him, "you'll be like a fly—you'll be swatted."

But Ibrahim still wouldn't budge. "Kill me today, then," he challenged them.

And to make absolutely sure everyone knew he had rejected Islam and was a fully committed follower of Christ, Ibrahim insisted on being baptized again—this time publicly. He asked members of his clan to come witness the event and personally invited twenty Muslim sheikhs.

That's the day he wrote his letter and oiled his handgun. Fortunately, neither was needed. Faith in Christ didn't mean he was incapable of sin, and Ibrahim admits that at times some of his old characteristics showed themselves. When God opened the door for Ibrahim to attend Bible school, he told Habiba to pack up and move with him. Though he's not proud of it now, he threatened to kill her if she refused. She agreed to go.

While in Bible school, Ibrahim got a taste of what it costs to share the gospel among Muslim Somalis. He and some classmates strapped loudspeakers to the top of Ibrahim's car and drove through Somali neighborhoods as Ibrahim preached.

They were often met with a hailstorm of rocks thrown by angry Muslims; occasionally, they were pulled from the car and beaten. Death threats were common, and more than once bullets tore through the sides of the car. Many of the Somali Muslims Ibrahim tried to reach were outraged. "If this man is really Somali, then he is an apostate," they said. "And apostates deserve death."

Ibrahim's car was even destroyed by an angry mob. Despite the opposition and death threats, he wasn't content to share the gospel only with Somalis in Kenya. He wanted to cross the border and tell more Somalis about Christ.

Because members of Ibrahim's clan lived both in Kenya and Somalia, it was easy for him to cross the border. He packed fifty New Testaments into white milk cans, strapped the cans to a camel, and headed out for a seven-day ride to Somalia.

Once he arrived, believers carefully disassembled the Bibles and distributed pages one at a time. Being caught with a Bible in Somalia could bring a death sentence. Four times a year, Ibrahim smuggled Bibles into Somalia, praying at each checkpoint that no one would think to open the cans.

On one occasion, he was arrested and held for four days before he was sent home.

Through the decades, as Ibrahim has faithfully shared the gospel, he's been shot, stoned, and arrested twice. But that persecution pales in comparison to what his clan did in an attempt to silence him: they took his wife and children away.

Habiba didn't want to go, but she couldn't oppose the relatives who wished to punish her "infidel" husband. For three years, she and the children lived as "guests" at the Saudi Arabian embassy in Nairobi. They weren't allowed to leave, and Ibrahim wasn't allowed inside. Though separated by just a few meters, they may as well have been living on different planets.

In all, Ibrahim was forcibly separated from his wife for a total of eleven years after he came to know Christ. Habiba was living with relatives when she died. She was buried before Ibrahim was even notified his wife of more than sixty years had passed away.

His comfort comes from time in God's Word and the body of Christ.

One passage that sustains Ibrahim is Psalm 5, which talks of God's care for his children and his punishment of those who abuse them. Matthew 25 speaks loudly to Ibrahim too—it reminds him to faithfully stay the course.

Though bent with age, Ibrahim still has a passion for sharing the gospel—especially with ethnic Somalis. And northern Kenya is dotted with living memorials of his work; he has planted twenty-three churches over the course of his ministry.

Pressure and persecution have hindered but never stopped Ibrahim's ministry. From preaching through loudspeakers, to smuggling Bibles, to passing along what he's learned in Bible schools and seminaries, he remains faithful in serving and sharing God's Word.

Ibrahim's church denomination specifies a mandatory retirement age for ministers, a number he passed long ago. But as long as God gives him strength, Ibrahim has no intention of retiring from sharing the gospel. "I cannot retire from the work of God," he said.

He remains as ready to preach and to share as he has ever been. And he is still ready to risk everything for the sake of seeing Somalis receive salvation through faith in Christ alone.

One of Ibrahim's favorite passages is from Matthew 25, in which Christ shared the Parable of the Talents. The master told the good servants, "Well done, good and faithful servant. You have been faithful over a little; I will set you over much. Enter the joy of your master" (verses 21, 23).

God has entrusted biblical disciples to be faithful in fulfilling the Great Commission. Each of the qualities we have seen in the lives of persecuted Christians facing Islamic extremism is necessary for the advancement of Christ in our world.

How are you inspired to sacrifice, live courageously, embrace joy, persevere, forgive like Christ, and be faithful in order to be a part of seeing the Great Commission fulfilled?

QUESTIONS FOR REFLECTION AND DISCUSSION

FAITHFULNESS

1. How would you define "faithfulness"? As you think of someone who is faithful to you, what are some of the defining characteristics that foster faithfulness?

2. Read Hebrews 10:23.

   a. What is a recent testimony you can recall where God displayed his faithfulness to you? Take a moment to share this with others in your family, class, or group. (Option: The group facilitator can pass out index cards and have those present write their brief testimony anonymously.)

   b. What comes to mind as you think of your own ability to hold fast to the confession of your hope without wavering? What is one situation you can recall where you displayed your faithfulness to God? Take a moment to share with

others in your family, class, or group. (Option: The group
facilitator can read the anonymous cards collected above.)

3. Zamira and Atamurat faced constant surveillance, harassment,
   police raids, fines, warnings, arrests, and interrogations. The
   continuous persecution affected their health and their ability
   to minister as they desired.

   a. What did you learn about God's faithfulness to them?

   b. What did you learn about their faithfulness to God?

   c. Zamira prayed, "I choose to be faithful, but I don't know
      how much more of this I can take." Do you agree or dis-
      agree with the statement that faithfulness, for the biblical
      disciple, is a choice? Why or why not?

   d. Even in prison, Atamurat was faithful to boldly share
      Christ with Muslims. Was that a choice? What could he
      have done instead? Why did he choose to be bold in his
      faith? How was God faithful to Atamurat while he was
      imprisoned?

   e. How does this story inspire your own choices to live as
      a faithful biblical disciple? Pray for your own ability to
      choose faithfulness—no matter the situation you face—
      and pray for those working on the frontlines of ministry
      like Atamurat and Zamira.

4. Where do you think our strength to choose faithfulness comes
   from? Explain.

   a. Read Ephesians 3:14–19.

b. As Paul (the author of Ephesians) prays for his fellow
     believers, what is he praying for them to be granted, to
     have, and to know in the following verses?

     verse 16

     verse 17

     verse 18

     verse 19

c. How would the things you listed above in verses 16–19
     foster faithfulness? Which of the things you identified
     would move you toward a greater level of faithfulness to
     God? Why?

d. How does being "strengthened through his Spirit" enable
     biblical disciples to be faithful?

e. What do you think Paul meant when he prayed, "that you
     may be filled with all the fullness of God" (verse 19)?

Pray

Take a moment to write a prayer or—if you are in a family, class, or
group—to pray sentence prayers that express gratitude to God for
his faithfulness, and that offer words of commitment that express
your desire to choose faithfulness to God. Also, as you close your
prayer, pray for our persecuted Christian family, that they will
remain faithful in the face of persecution from Islamic extremists.

COMMITMENT

Stories That Provoked a Response

These stories have taken us to places such as Egypt, Iran, Nigeria, Iraq, and Pakistan. We have seen biblical themes of sacrifice, courage, joy, perseverance, forgiveness, and faithfulness. The experiences of Samrita, Musa, Amina, Fenny, Nadia, Dereje, Walid, Alejandro, Emily, and Ibrahim are current and real, and they have inspired us.

We have read about the tears of these persecuted family members and perhaps even wept along with them. We have seen their joy and felt the hope that only an eternal perspective offers following the devastation they have faced. Their stories compel us to ask ourselves, "What does it mean for *me* to be 'n' where I live?"

We need their example of faithfulness in the face of persecution. Their sacrifices are a powerful testimony to our loving God, whose grace reaches out to save every sinner and empowers those who follow Jesus to live in faithful service to him.

The pattern of joy they manifest as they persevere and courageously serve Jesus inspires us and equips us to do the same. God is with those who are persecuted in a special, intimate way. As we lift them in prayer, God gives us the privilege of being his hands, feet, and voices alongside them, no matter where we live.

What Is Your Response? Are You "N"?

You may be wondering how you would respond if you faced direct persecution. You may wonder if you would represent Christ well. We want to assure you that you *do* have everything you need to respond well. If you have Christ, you have everything you need.

In Luke 21:12–15, Jesus taught his disciples to prepare for persecution. He said, "But before all this they will lay their hands on you and persecute you, delivering you up to the synagogues and prisons, and you will be brought before kings and governors for my name's sake. This will be your opportunity to bear witness. Settle it therefore in your minds not to meditate beforehand how to answer, for I will give you a mouth and wisdom, which none of your adversaries will be able to withstand or contradict."

As a biblical disciple, we can be confident in this: no matter what we are facing, no matter where we find ourselves, no matter what kind of enemy we encounter, he will guide us—even the words that come out of our mouths. The promise is clear. God will be with you, and as you depend on him, he will guide you.

However, we need to decide today and every day to grow in our relationship with the Lord by spending time in his Word and in prayer. We also need to be in regular fellowship with a body of believers and intentionally share our faith with the lost. The personal discipleship you pursue each day will help equip you to face opposition for your faith as you bear witness for Christ.

Now that you have been introduced to your brothers and sisters in some of the world's most difficult and dangerous places to follow Christ, God will lead you to pray for them and to serve them. Our unity as members—one with another—in the global body of Christ demands standing with persecuted Christians in fellowship. As we pray for them, they will be strengthened. We, in turn, will draw strength from their victories and learn from their examples.

We will keep our eyes fixed on our eternal hope in Christ, knowing that he is with us and that we are part of his eternal kingdom.

Our God is faithful. He will be with us, and his Great Commission will be accomplished!

I AM N
COMMITMENT
PRAYER

Heavenly Father,

I have been inspired by my persecuted Christian brothers and sisters, and I ask that you empower me to take active steps so I can grow in:

- SACRIFICE. I will count the cost of discipleship and willingly pay the price because you are worth it.
- COURAGE. I will not be paralyzed by fear because you empower me as I take risks to witness for you.
- JOY. I will rejoice in the midst of my struggles and suffering in this world because of the eternal hope I have in you.
- PERSEVERANCE. I will stand firm, resisting any opposition. By your strength, I will endure and overcome.

- FORGIVENESS. I will allow you to work in my heart as I obey you by loving my enemies and forgiving others as you have forgiven me.
- FAITHFULNESS. I will not allow adversity to cause me to be unfaithful to your Word or disobedient to your purposes.

Lord, help me be mindful of my Christian brothers and sisters so I will never let them suffer in silence, nor will I let them serve alone. I will let their testimonies inspire me to follow you. *I am n.*

_____   _____

NAME   DATE

i-am-n.com

Areas Where Christians Face Islamic Extremists

Select Groups and Hotspots

1. **Kenya & Somalia**
   Al-Shabab

2. **Nigeria, Niger, Cameroon, & Chad**
   Islamic State of West Africa Province (ISWAP) and Boko Haram

3. **Iraq & Syria**
   The Islamic State (IS) (ISIS/ISIL)

4. **Egypt**
   The Muslim Brotherhood

5. **Yemen**
   Al-Qaida

6. **Philippines**
   Moro National/Islamic Liberation Front, Abu Sayyaf

7. **Afghanistan & Pakistan**
   The Taliban & Islamic State (Khorasan Province)

8. **Sudan**
   Islamist government leaders and factions

9. **Algeria, Tunisia, & Libya**
   Al-Qaida and Ansar al-Shariahe

10. **Mozambique**
    ISIS - Mozambique

11. **Democratic Republic of Congo (DRC) & Uganda**
    Allied Democratic Forces, an affiliate of ISIS

12. **Mali & Burkina Faso**
    Jamaat Nusrat Al-Islam wal Muslimeen (JNIM) and Islamic State (IS)

13. **Ethiopia**
    ISIS and Al-Shabab affiliates

To learn more, visit vom.org/cfie.

ABOUT THE VOICE
OF THE MARTYRS

The Voice of the Martyrs (VOM) is a missionary organization dedicated to serving persecuted Christians in the world's most difficult and dangerous places to follow Christ, while inspiring all members of the global body of Christ to enter into fellowship with one another. VOM was founded in 1967 by Pastor Richard Wurmbrand (1909–2001) and his wife, Sabina (1913–2000). Richard was imprisoned fourteen years in Communist Romania for his faith in Christ, and Sabina was imprisoned for three years. Soon after their imprisonment, they founded VOM and established a family of missions dedicated to assisting persecuted Christians worldwide.

To be inspired by the bold faith of our persecuted brothers and sisters in Christ who are working to advance the gospel in hostile areas and restricted nations, request a free subscription to VOM's award-winning monthly magazine. Visit us at vom.org, or call 800-747-0085.

To learn more about VOM's work, please contact us:

United States	vom.org
Australia	vom.com.au
Belgium	hvk-aem.be
Brazil	maisnomundo.org
Canada	vomcanada.com
Czech Republic	hlas-mucedniku.cz
Finland	marttyyrienaani.fi
Germany	verfolgte-christen.org
The Netherlands	sdok.nl
New Zealand	vom.org.nz
Poland	gpch.pl
Portugal	vozdosmartires.com
Singapore	gosheninternational.org
South Africa	persecutionsa.org
South Korea	vomkorea.kr
United Kingdom	releaseinternational.org

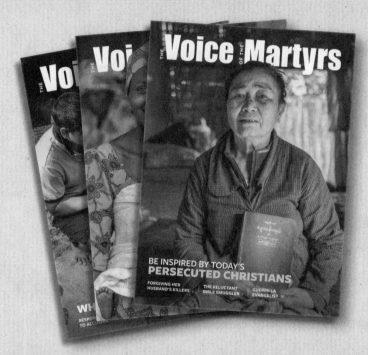

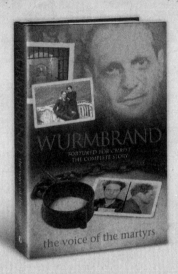

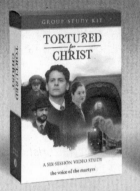 

GET THE FULL STORY

Richard and Sabina Wurmbrand, founders of The Voice of the Martyrs, boldly witnessed for Christ amid Nazi and Communist oppression in Romania. Their full story can now be experienced for free in two award-winning feature films.

Tortured for Christ — The Movie

This is a cinematic retelling of VOM founder Richard Wurmbrand's testimony, as written in his international bestseller *Tortured for Christ*. Filmed entirely in Romania, including in the very prison where Richard endured torture and solitary confinement, this powerful film will challenge every viewer to consider what it means to sacrifice for following Jesus Christ.

Sabina: Tortured for Christ, the Nazi Years

See how God's love transformed an ambitious, atheistic hedonist into one of the greatest Christian women of the 20th century. After Nazis killed her entire family, Sabina Wurmbrand risked her own life to share the love and truth of Christ with them. Experience the amazing true story that has inspired millions around the world.

To view both movies on-demand for free, visit
vom.org/WurmbrandMovies.

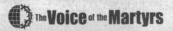

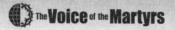